# BLACK SMOKE
and
*Peanut Butter Sandwiches*

## Valerie Huffman Osborn

Mayhaven Publishing, Inc.

P O Box 557

Mahomet, IL 61853

USA

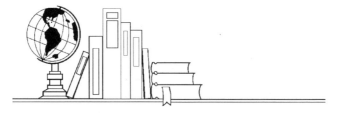

Cover Design by Michael Osborn

Copyright © 2012 Valerie Huffman Osborn

Library of Congress Cataloging Number: 2012932915

First Edition—First Printing 2012

ISBN 13 978 193227881-1

ISBN 10 193227881-8

# Dedication

Within these pages are stories from the life and the times of an only child. Although some of the people's names and places may be fictitious, the stories are based on real-life experiences. I hope you can glean some hope, joy, tears and happiness from this book. This one is for you, dear Mom and Dad, Donna and Owen, Michael and Kim and our grandchildren.

And in memory of Betty Osborn, Mary Heckman, Pat Lamb, and dear friends Kay Longshaw, Tepa Mostert, Betty Nicholas and Sherron Bodamer.

# Contents

Mildred (Kirkpatrick) Huffman and Glenn Huffman
Their Wedding Day—1939.

# In the Beginning

*In* the beginning there was a young man and a young woman. They lived not to far away from each other in the county of Vermillion.

The young man was a handsome one. Glenn came from a farm background. His father was well known in the community and had a reputation for his kindness and work ethics. His mother was a strong-willed woman—and you knew she ruled the roost. Glenn was a hard-working young man.

As a young boy he would work in the field with his dad. Sometimes he would bring lunch out to his father. It was on such an occasion he'd gone out to help his father. His dad was just unhooking the plow horses when Glenn arrived. He didn't know his father had unhooked the horses to send them home. He thought they needed to be hooked up, so he started to hook them back up when his dad wasn't looking and somehow the horses got spooked and took off. Glenn was under the cupeling part when the horses took off.

He was wearing suspenders, and one of them got caught on the plow and started to drag him along with it. This was very dangerous. If the plow hit a rock, it could have cut him—badly. As fate or a higher power would have it, the horses reached a ditch right before the road, jumped it and as Glenn hit the edge of the ditch his suspender broke and he landed in the ditch. The horses were already almost home when Glenn's dad found him, no less for the wear, though a bit bruised. By the time they got back to the homestead the horses were already at the barn. It would seem the angels were watching over this young lad. He was in store for a long, creative and interesting life.

The young woman was from a small farm, with a stern father, a sweet mother and three siblings. She was the oldest, slender, small framed and rather fragile looking. Mildred was her name, and she is my mother. She had been born during WW I in times of dire stress. Grandpa was overseas fighting in Germany. He was so close to the front lines that he could hear and smell the firing of the guns. Grandpa Kirkpatrick said, as the men were marching back—some torn and bloody, some carrying their dead with them—Grandpa and his buddy were on their way up to the very front lines. Scared at the sight of it all made it even more surreal. Just as Grandpa and the soldiers were almost there, the news came that the War was over. The Armistice had been signed. Great relief filled each man, as they turned around and marched back to safety.

It was during this time that Grandma was under such stress and that Mildred was born—a premature baby. In those days, most premies didn't make it. She was so tiny they had to carry her on a pillow. But she survived. As she grew up she suffered many health problems. A fighter, it seemed, no matter what the problem, Mom survived. And she has survived for all these years. In January of 2012, she celebrated her ninety-third birthday.

The next in line to be born was her sister Lucille. The two went through The Great Depression wearing whatever their mother made them and sometimes being made fun of by their classmates because of their homespun clothing or strange combinations. I remember Mother telling me of a time when Grandma found some bright, yellow-green stockings. Much to the disappointment of both sisters, they were given the socks to wear to school. Even though their dresses were longer, those socks stood out like sore thumbs on them and the children at school made fun of them, calling them, "Chicken Legs." Mom said she just hated those socks and I know that was a color she would never, ever wear again—and she hasn't.

Children can be cruel, unthinking, and say hurtful things. We see it everyday—even now—causing great pain in lives that would be otherwise be happy. We should be more careful how we treat others. In this case the Bible says, "Do unto others as you would have them do unto you." Perhaps that's something that should be posted in every school, in every public hall of every country. It might not make a difference now, but could in the future. My mother was lucky. She went on to a whole new life with my father.

After Lucille came Ray, who grew to be taller than Grandpa Kirkpatrick. He served in WW II—the same time Dad did. He later married, but died early in life from a heart attack. Ray was the one who would pick his nieces up and tease us, saying he would throw us in the horse tank. Of course he never did, but it was always fun trying to run away, and being swooped up by him.

After Ray, came Dora. She was a bright and happy person and married Dad's best Army buddy Jake. They made a home near Grandpa Kirkpatrick's. They had a long life together until he died a few years ago. The thing I noticed most about Aunt Dora is her wonderful sense of humor, and I still love talking with her.

At left:
Ray Kirkpatrick.

At Right:
Mildred, Lucille and
Dora Kirkpatrick
in high school during
the 1930s.

# An Only Child

Being an only child can have its pluses and its drawbacks. In my early years it was just Dad, Mom and me. We lived in a small house in Danville. Dad worked at the shoe factory, and Mom had worked at the box factory, In fact, that's how they met. His sister worked at the box factory, too, and knew Mom. She introduced they two of them, and after a time of dating, Dad asked Mom to marry him. Her father was a strict man, so when dad was presented to him there was some questions asked. When he found out that Dad was the son of C. Huffman he was impressed. The Huffmans were considered well set. Grandpa Kirkpatrick was also a respected man, but was not as well set as the Huffmans. Grandma Kirkpatrick was a woman of great strength and compassion. As for Grandma Huffman, she was a woman you didn't want to cross. She was a strong-willed woman and definitely ruled the House of Huffman.

Great-grandma Stella
and Great-grandpa Clarence Huffman
1920s.

I was born in 1941, and due to a hard labor, the stupidity of nurses and a doctor that couldn't make it on time to the delivery, the birth went badly, and Mother would no longer be able to have any more children. About seven months after I came along, so did the bombing of Pearl Harbor and life for us, for a few years, would be so completely different.

By 1943, Dad was called to serve in the military. He chose the Army Air Corp. In those days the Army and Air Force were all together. It meant that Dad would be gone from us much of the time. Dad finished his boot camp in Rantoul, Illinois, where there was an Army Air Force Base. We went to live with Grandma and Grandpa Kirkpatrick.

After boot camp, Dad was shipped off to some place and then to Amarillo, Texas, where Mom and I were to meet him. That's where the feathers hit the fan. Mom decided to go with him on the train. I was there, although I don't remember all the hairy things that happened. Mom said we got on the train and as they got settled in she realized she was the only woman on that train. All the other spouses of soldiers had decided to travel on a civilian train. To her surprise, when the train pulled in to a little tiny train station, out in the middle of nowhere, she was at a loss of what to do. She was told she couldn't go with Dad and the other men, and that she would have to wait at the train station until someone could come get her (and me). The men had to be put, through a time of adjustment, and quarters for them still had to be arranged.

Well, there we were, sitting on our suitcases, a very sad woman and a very small child of three who was fussy. There was no way to get to town, and there was no one at the station to help her. The station was out in a cow pasture that went on for miles and all around us, were steers and cows. Hey, it was Texas, wide open spaces, tumbleweed and hot.

After a few hours, along came the mail carrier. He saw the predicament we were in and even though it was most likely unlawful, he picked up our suitcases and we climbed into his little truck and off we went to

Amarillo to find Dad.

When we got there, we found no Dad—no husband, and we were left off at a small hotel where Mom had just enough money to get us a room and a little food to eat. She tried to call the base, but by that time it was late at night and she was told she would have to call back the next day. Scared, and very unhappy with her circumstance, she put me to bed and finally we both went to sleep. Of course Dad had no idea where we were and the next morning he called around to the different hotels and finally found us. At last we were united as a family again and life at the air-force base began for us. It took courage and fortitude for that tiny woman to get through 24 exhausting hours of worry—and yet knowing all would be well. Seeing Dad, again, is what got her through it. Sometimes it only takes a little thing like this to be thankful for those who put out that helping hand. I know, though we never saw him again, and I've always wondered what happened to our angel of a mail carrier.

Here I am.
Three-year-old Valerie Huffman.

# Living in a Chicken Coup

After we arrived at the Army Air Force base in Amarillo, we were told that housing would be available for us. Mom thought it had to be better than the room at the hotel, but when she saw what we would have to live in, I'm sure she cried. Our "home" was no more than a chicken coup converted to a small house. It was drafty, buggy and downright disgusting to her. She knew she was not going to like Texas at all, and yet here she was and would have to remain, until Dad was transferred somewhere else. After all, it was this or be separated from him and head back home to her parents place. So she chose to weather it out. After all, she was the wife of an Airman and it just wouldn't do to leave him. That was so unheard of in those days. You stood by your man no matter where he went. Mother was resourceful, and with a bit of cheap material she made curtains that brightened up the dull place. We endured the hot weather and the bitter cold of the Texas winters. I don't remember much about this time, but I do remember that we did go back to Illinois for a short time, as we were on our way back, I came down with Whooping Cough. This put even more on Mom. She was by herself and if it hadn't been for another guardian angel coming along I think she might have lost it. She said I coughed so much I turned blue. Fortunately, there was a soldier who was going home for a visit. He held me so Mom could rest. It was the train ride from...—well, you know what I mean—as far as she was concerned. At the other end of the line—in Danville—waited Grandfather Kirkpatrick. He'd gotten wind of the problem and drove to the station to pick Mom up rather than make her deal with anything else. No wonder she hated trains.

Over time, I got well and we returned to Texas to be with Dad. Sometimes we still speak of it, of enduring to the end. The end of each of our experiences—be it good or bad—helps us endure through the next experience, and that is a good thing. It makes us stronger and, hopefully, wiser.

# Trainburgers

On one of our trips across the wide open spaces of our country, we were seated on another train. It was the one that would take us as far as Houston, Texas, and from there we were to go by bus to Galveston. The train was full of all kinds of passengers. We chugged out of the train station at a good steady pace. The scenery changed as we traveled through each state. Mom said we had quite a trip.

Everything was going well. The train was on its way to our destination. I think we must have fallen asleep for a while, because when we woke up the train suddenly came to a screeching stop. There seemed to be a problem on the track. When Mom looked out the window all she could see were the dead bodies of cattle. They were scattered everywhere along the track. When one of the passengers asked what had happened, he was told by the conductor that the train couldn't stop quick enough and had hit a heard of cattle that was crossing the tracks. It took quite awhile before help came to take care of the mess as they had to call a cleanup crew to come out and remove the dead bodies.

Mom said the smell was atrocious and everyone on the train lost their appetite. After many hours, when they finally did underway, it was at a slower pace as night had fallen. I think, for a long time, many who witness the sight would not eat hamburgers for a while. I know Mom said she didn't feel like it. As for me, I don't think it really mattered. I still like hamburgers with pickle, mustard, lettuce and tomato, but not on a sesame seed bun!

Mom, Dad and me as a World War II family.

# Hurricanes and Mosquitoes

During the time, when I was three or four years old, my father was stationed at the Army Air Force in Galveston. We'd come there to be with him and lived in a three-story apartment building. The days were hot and breezy near the ocean and the nights were hot and humid, and the mosquitoes were unbelievable.

In the daytime, Mom would take me down to the beach, which we were near, and I would enjoy playing, building little sand castles, and Mom would relax and enjoy the warm sun under an umbrella.

At night time, though, it was another story. It seemed, the mosquitoes would come out of the woodwork. They loved preying on me, and Mom said I was just so bitten up I would just scatch and scratch. You see, in the 1940s they didn't have much of anything to ward off the little buggers. She would put some stinky powder on me and rub on some camphor oil that really stunk.

Four years old in Texas.

Then one day, when we were out and about the area, the wind began to pick up and some ugly clouds started forming. Mom said we'd better get back to the apartment. Those clouds look really bad and we need to be inside. Much to my dismay we went back to the apartment. I'd really looked forward to playing in the sand.

When we got home the telephone rang. It was Dad calling. He told us there was a hurricane on its way and it was too late to get us back to the base, but that he could make it to the apartment. When he arrived, the wind had really began to howl and the rain had started. As the storm approached the wind picked up even more, and soon we were right in the middle of a horrendous storm. Dad and Mom had put me in my crib. We were on the top level of the apartment building and the structure would sway back and forth with the wind. Dad said my little bed would go from one side of the room to the other—unless they held on to it. They were sure the building would be toppled, but it held up fairly well.

When the storm was over, and we heard the all clear, we ventured down the flight of stairs that led to the ground floor only to find it deep in water. We were stuck for another day.

After a few days, Mom took me back out to the beach. I was looking forward to playing in the sun. What we found was a mess! There was all kinds of things on the beach: dead fish, seaweed, pieces of wood, nasty black tar, that if you stepped in it, you had a hard time getting it off. Mom told me to watch where I stepped, "Good grief, I sure don't want to have to clean tar off you!" But it was darn hard not to get it on one or the other of my little sandals and I most likely did, as she scolded me after we came back from the beach.

Sometimes in life we have storms, and mosquitoes that 'bug,' us, and we have to walk through a little tar along the way. As long was we watch where we step, we're safe. The trick is to stay on the safe road to help us get through life.

# The Crawdad Hole

When I was a little girl of about eight, it was always fun to run off down to the local country bridge and fish for crawdads. It was just a strong wooden bridge with a railing on it. Now, Mom always told me not to go unless Grandpa Kirkpatrick could go along. I guess she was afraid I'd fall off the bridge, or fall into the small stream that ran under it. But there was a hole just off from the bridge that I knew, as did most of us kids in the area, where a big old granddaddy of a crayfish we called Big Joe could be found, just sitting there, taunting us all to come and get him. He would come out and sun himself in the warm water and then, just as you thought you had your line close, and you had a chance of getting him, he would take the bait right off the line and scamper off. I was determined to get that old guy. *Yes, today,* I told myself, *You, Val, are going to get that stinkin' old thing and you're going to outwit him and catch him.*

I had my trusty pole Grandpa Kirkpatrick had cut for me off a tree, and a line with a sturdy safety pin to hold the bait. I even had the old crawdaddy's favorite bait—bread mixed with bacon grease and chilled to harden. I was sure to catch the wily old guy.

I sat down on the edge of the bridge—just waiting. Pretty soon, here came my cousin Eva. She had the same idea, as she came with a pole her dad had made for her.

We said our Hi's and she sat down to get her pole ready. We both agreed that with two of us after that old crawdad he was sure to be the trophy we wanted to see. We threw our lines in and waited, and waited—and waited. It was a quite a wait because we knew if we got to talkin' we would scare him off. Just when we thought nothing was going to happen, here came Old Joe. He was a little slower than I remember him as he made his way to his favorite spot in the creek.

The lines were ready and so were we. Under our breaths, we both were saying, "Come on you ol' bugger. Come to my line." Then as if he'd heard her, he slowly crawled over to Eva's line and promptly pulled off her bait with one quick swoop. Then he swam to my line. *Oh*, I thought, *come and get it. I'm ready for you.*

Just as he clamped down on my line, I gave him a big jerk and he went flyin' over my head. He flew up and then to the other side of the bridge where he dangled.

"Oh you got him," Eva shouted.

Yes. It appeared I had caught the wiley creature. As I reeled him in, I was elated, then I remembered all the stories everyone told about how they'd almost caught him. Now, there would never again be an Old Joe to catch if I took him home. So with much care, I started to drop him back down toward the water.

"What in the dickens are you doing?" Eva yelled.

"I'm sorry, I just can't do it. What about all the other kids that want to catch him. Why he's like a legend around here, Eva. I've got to put him back. The fishin' hole will never be the same."

"Hmm," my cousin mumbled. "I can see your point, but you really did catch him, so we both know it, and you can tell Grandpa about it and he'll know it, too. Look, here he comes right now! He can be a witness to what you're about to do. Then he can confirm it to everyone else."

"Oh, alright. I'll wait," I sighed as I watch the crawdad wiggle at the end of my pole. Sure enough Grandpa did witness the letting go of Old Joe.

As we all walked away from the bridge, I swear I could almost here that crusty old crawdad say, "See you around." I smiled. I knew I would, someday.

Isn't that the way it is sometimes with temptation? It's always around the corner saying, "See You around." And you know it's something you can deal with as long as you have faith in something greater—whatever your belief may be.

Left to right: Me with cousins Patricia and Eva.

# Old Shake Rag School

Back in the early 1900s, there was a school built in our area near Bismarck. My grandmother attended there, as did my mother, and as I did. It was a little unusual in the mid-1940s that it was still standing as a one-room country school. This was a working school with classes from one through eight grades and a teacher that was like none you would see today. In those days the teacher ruled.

Her name was Miss Tutwiler and she was a bear when it came to strictness. There wasn't much that got past her. There were times when I swear that woman had eyes in the back of her head. Not only was she sharp as a tack, but she kept a ruler in her hand and a belt in her drawer in her desk.

There were two occasions when I remember her using that ruler. One was on me, and the other was on a child whose name I don't remember. We had writing time to practice our handwriting skills. You had three things to work with: lined paper, a fountain pen and an ink well to fill that pen up. In Mother's day they used an opened-end pen that you dipped into the ink. Well, on a particular day I was not feeling like practicing. I was being lazy and letting my o's look more like a's in my words—and Mrs. Tutwiler caught me. Before I had time to react, she came down on my hand with that ruler and said, "Lift that wrist, and curl that 'o' up more. This is the messiest I've ever seen. You'll stay after school today and practice o's until you get it right." Well, in those days we didn't have a phone, so I knew Mom and Dad would not be very happy that I had to stay after school. Boy, if you don't think that after that I really worked hard on those letters to get them right. I sure didn't want to feel the sting of that ruler on my hand again.

Of course through all of this there were giggles, and a loud, "Hush, children," as Mrs. Tutwiler strived to quiet the rest of the classes down.

Oh, how humiliated I felt.

But there were worse times. I saw her use the *belt* was on one of the Corry boys. They were mischievous kids and were always doing something to cause a commotion. On one of these occasions both the boys had decided it would be fun to hide everyone's lunches. So when noon came we went into the cloak room and our lunches were no where in sight. Well, just trying to find them would throw Mrs. Tutwiler's schedule off, and she soon caught on to what had happened. The two boys were in the back of the room, smirking at each other and looking very guilty at the same time.

"All right you two. Since you're the only ones who didn't go in the cloak room, you must know where the lunches are, so go get them and bring them in here." She raised her eyebrows and shoulders in authority that she always showed when she really meant it.

"We don't know what you are talking about," they chimed as they shrugged their shoulders and slunk down at their desks.

"Boys, there's only one way we can find out—and you know what that means." As she said that she walked up to the desk and pulled out the dreaded belt. Seeing what she was doing, both the boys tried to make a bee line for the door, but forgot it was always locked after everyone got into the school. There they were, with her one on side and a locked door on the other. About that time another one of the student, a rather large boy came out of the cloak room and grabbed one of the Corry boys and hauled him up to the front of the room, where Mrs. Tutwiler said, "Alright bend over. You know the punishment for lying and for your bad deed.

"Yes, um I shore do." The younger brother stood there—defiant. His older brother, who couldn't bear to see his little brother pay the price for the deed he'd roped him into—confessed. He then placed himself in between the teacher and his little brother and said, "I'll take the whipping, ma'am."

"No. You will both get a whipping. Neither of you will learn until you pay the price for your bad deed."

Both boys bent over and she gave the younger boy a good swat on the bottom and told him to sit down. As for the older one, it was a harder sounding "wap," and I'm sure it stung a bit. Both boys were forbidden to eat their lunches that day, and later the teacher visited their parents with a stern suggestion that both boys behave themselves or they wouldn't be going to *that* school anymore. Except for the Halloween incident (which involved more than one boy, both of the Corry kids behaved themselves pretty well at school. Today that school still stands—but now as a lovely home.

I look back on that incident and it reminds me of when we do things that are indiscretions and how in the scriptures the Lord steps in and says, "I've taken care of that for you. Go, my son and sin no more. I've taken your place.'

# Worms—Mmmm Good

Did you ever have a kid in school that just got to you? You know the kind, the one who always teases you, bullies you and just plain makes life miserable.

When I was a young girl, my friend and I knew a boy who just wouldn't leave us alone—especially at lunch time. We would have to hide to eat our lunch. One day we had noticed that he wasn't anywhere near us, so we sat down on a bench near the playground to eat. No sooner had we opened up our lunch boxes than here he came. My friend said to me, "Well here we go again. Another lunch lost!"

Later that afternoon on our play break, I talked with my friend and we both agreed something had to be done! We were tired of being taken advantage of, so we devised a plan. In fact I thought it was a rather ingenious idea.

The next day, during morning break we went out to the back of the school where there were not many kids and we dug up a couple of worms. We stuck them in between a peanut butter and jelly sandwich and wrapped them up as nice and neat as we could.

That day at noon, while we were sitting on the swings eating our lunch, sure enough here he came. We knew what he wanted and we waited until he came up to us and said, "All right, hand over your food, I'm really hungry today."

"Oh do we have to?" I said with a sad look.

"Yeah, and be quick about it or I'll mash that little lunch box of yours—along with your friend's."

"Oh, All right, be that way," I said, and reached into my lunch box and reluctantly handed over my sandwich, along with some extra cookies I'd brought. Well, I figured I had to make it look good.

He sat down on the ground and unwrapped the sandwich. We watched with great expectation and weren't disappointed. As he bit into that nice, juicy peanut butter, worm and jelly sandwich, he frowned, feeling something gritty. We hadn't exactly had time to wash the worms off, so we'd just thrown them into the sandwich as is. He chewed the first bit and went to take another one—and then he saw them. Those wiggly worms were laying in that yummy, gooey peanut butter. He screamed so loud it brought the other children running. He spit out the sandwich and all of a sudden got a strange look on his face. He ran to the end of the schoolyard and began to up chuck.

Everyone wanted to know what had happened. All we said was that he'd eaten something that hadn't agreed with him. We carefully picked up the dropped sandwich and threw it onto the trash, went back to our own lunches and thoroughly enjoyed them that day and every day after that. You see, he never bothered us again. The rest of the school year he stayed away from us, making a point of leaving us alone.

There's the old saying: "Never bite off more than you can chew." In this case you might want to say, "Never bite into another man's sandwich. You never know what might lie below the surface."

# Lilacs and Hollyhocks

Along the side of my grandparents rock driveway, sat several Lilac bushes. In the spring, they would green up and then the blooms would come. The fragrance wafted through the air, all around. You could sit on their front porch and take in, not only the beauty of the flowers, but the fragrance that lingered with you even after leaving their place.

Grandma would often cut some, bring them in and place them on her kitchen table—as would my mother. There always seemed something comforting about those lilacs. Maybe it was the inviting fragrance or their beauty. Maybe it was because they were at Grandma's.

My cousin and I would go out and sit on a blanket in the front yard with a handful of those flowers and smell them until our noses were just full of their scent. They also blocked out the smell of the pigs and other livestock that wondered around on the other side of the fence—just beyond the lilac bushes.

Years later, after we'd moved away, we came back to visit Grandpa and Grandma Kirkpatrick. The bushes were still there and again we would take in the wonderful fragrance. We would cut some to take home with us in a jar of water so they would remain fresh.

A couple years ago we drove down that road and turned into the same driveway, now abandoned. The property was in shambles with weeds and brush growing all around. We had been there before when we had gotten the water from the spring well. As if by magic though, there were the same lilac bushes, now covered with wild vines, but still producing those wonderful flowers.

As I got out of the car my the scent immediately conjured up lovely memories associated was Grandma and Grandpa Kirkpatrick's home. We walked around the property and before we left I went over and cut some of those lilacs. I knew they wouldn't last very long, but for a short time I had something of Grandma, again.

Now for hollyhocks, those wonderful tall, colorful flowers which grew by the fence line. We, as children, adored playing with them. They weren't just flowers. They were dancing dolls and water princesses. It was amazing to us what you could do with a toothpick and the bud and flower of the hollyhock. With the single effort of sticking the toothpick into the bud, linking the rest into the flower we had a real flower girl. We would take them to the horse tank, or little stream that ran nearby, and let them float on the water. We would push them around, and make them dance on the water and we'd see who could win a race by blowing on them.

I doubt, today, there are very many little girls that even know about lilacs and hollyhocks. It's so sad, in this day of texting and twittering, that children can't take the time to find the fun in simple things that nature and life offers.

Today, I have my own little lilac bush that I can enjoy. And I hope I can share it's fragrance and beauty with my grandchildren someday.

We're so blessed sometimes with these sweet memories. They can also be a source of sadness for times gone by, and remind us that times to come may not be so kind to us. As a saying might goes, "In the garden of life we are given both the weeds and the flowers. It's up to us to dispose of the bad and to enjoy the fragrance of the good."

# The Hill

When I was a young girl, I walked to the Shake Rag School that sat on Shake Rag Road. It was about a half-a-mile walk one way. In the winter it was cold, but Mom always bundled me up and off I would go—meeting up with my two cousins. We'd try not to goof-off, but as spring would come, it was more fun to walk slower to both home and school.

In the winter, with snowball fights and sliding up and down the hill we had to walk by, was so much fun. I remember when one of the boys, walking along with us, hadn't brought his sled. So, he decided to slide down the hill on his lunch tin. You could say it was anything but great would be an understatement. It was funny, though, but he ended up with a crunched lunchbox he'd have to explain to his mom.

In the spring and fall, we'd take our shoes off and wade in the tiny stream that flowed at the bottom of the hill. Wild flowers were a great treasure to take home to our mothers, and sometimes we would try to take short cuts that we weren't supposed to. We even picked berries that grew near by. My cousin and I would cut through the fields, taking chances that we weren't caught and yelled at by our dads or our neighbors.

One day one of my cousins tried to ride her bike up the hill really fast and the bicycle got away from her and down she went. When we got to her there was a small chunk of flesh that had been taken out of her knee. My other cousin couldn't bear to look at it as the wound bleed freely. She was one of those people that fainted at the sight of blood and was about to do so. All I knew was that it had to be covered, so I took a bandana and tied it over the wound. I kept looking for the piece of flesh that had been taken out. I guess I thought if we could find it, a doctor could sew it back on. Silly me. We got my cousin home and her mother urged us to go home. We were already late and I hadn't noticed that there was some blood on my jeans where it hadn't been when I helped my cousin. *Boy,* I thought, *Mom will really be mad when she sees this.*

When I got home I didn't say anything to Mom, but went to change my jeans and tried to wash out the blood. I threw the dirty jeans into the laundry basket and went to help Dad with some chores that I was late in doing. I don't remember what happened after that. I just know that we were a lot more careful getting up and over that hill.

That same gravel road has been replaced by a smoother road, and the little stream that ran under the tiny bridge at the foot of the hill seems much smaller.

We all have hills to climb. Some of them bigger than others, and some are just a breeze. What keeps us going is what's on the other side of the hill. Our innate drive to conquer, to go forth with courage, our curiosity and just plain stubbornness to try something new, drives us, even though at times it would seem those hills in our lives were are insurmountable—we keep on trying.

The song *Climb every Mountain*, says it all. We were innocent children seeing only the joy and fun in climbing that hill. As adults, we sometimes need to climb our hills or mountains with the same attitude as a child would, with faith, joy and a drive that gets us to the other side.

Valerie Huffman Osborn

# Water Pumps and Icicles

In our backyard sat a pump for a drilled well and tapped into good spring water below. It was our only source of water, and we all took turns pumping that water into buckets and taking them into the house. Now this may seem like I'm talking about the 1800s, but this was from 1948 to 1950 when we lived in the country. It was hard hauling that water into the house, and I knew Mom and I got tired of it—as did Dad. In the summer it was hot, and in the winter sometimes the pump would freeze. Dad would have to prime it to get it to work. There was an occasion when it had rained first and then turned to snow. The handle of the pump froze over with icicles hanging down. It was so much fun to lick those icicles. Well,I went out to get water and—you know how sometimes you just do something just plain silly? I did it. I leaned down to lick that cold ice and My tongue got stuck. I mean it really stuck—to the handle!

I couldn't scream. You can't scream stuck to ice. Finally one of my parents looked out the window wondering why I hadn't come back to the house and saw me flailing about like a chicken with its head off. They ran outside and gently poured some tepid water over the ice to loosen my tongue. Boy! What a relief when it came off. Of course Mom told me how silly I was, "Now I hope you've learned a lesson, I hope you'll never try that stunt again."

My tongue was sore for a few days, but I recovered, as did my wounded pride. I was careful about which icicles I licked after that

A few years later, Dad put in a new kitchen sink and layed a line from the well to the house so we could have running water. The old pump disappeared, and with it the temptation to lick those icicles.

Just like the temptation to lick those icicles we're tempted everyday with all kinds of things. The trick is to not let them get at us. Using restraint, when something or someone entices us to try something new that could lead to our downfall, will keep us safe from the icicles of temptation. Might I also say here that praying, no matter what faith we are, can help defeat those icicles that hang in our way of getting to a goal we might have. No matter what our icicles of temptation might be, remember the story of the water pump and don't get stuck!

# A Dangerous Lunch Bucket

When my husband was a little boy, no more than five or six, his mother took him and his sisters shopping for school supplies. It was a new school year and this was his first time there. She bought him a new lunch bucket and he was overjoyed at the prospect of being able to use it.

They all got back to the car and jumped in. Paul was in the back seat with one of his sisters. Now, this was in the 1930s when cars didn't have seatbelts. It was an old Packard whose doors opened up backwards. They started down the road and even though it was an early fall day, it had gotten hotter than usual. Paul had worn his winter coat that day because his mom had insisted it was a bit chilly that morning. The car was going along at a moderate speed when Paul decided to roll down the window because he was hot. Well, he got hold of the wrong handle and the door flew open taking him with it. The next thing he knew, he'd hit the pavement with a thud and was dragged for a couple of feet before he let go.

He lay there for a few moments only to realize that his mom was leaving him behind. Even though he was scraped up a bit, and had a little less hair on his head, he started to run after the car. His sisters were so engrossed in their school supplies, that at first they didn't realize what had happened. Then his sister Elizabeth hollered at their mom and imagine the surprise when his mom looked up in the rear-view mirror and saw Paul, there, in the middle of the road!

It was a good thing that there had been no other cars on the road that day. She put on the brakes and gently backed the car up and got out and ran to where JR was. Although he was a bit banged up, and had lost a bit of hair from the back of his head—he had no broken bones.

They all got back into the car and their mom made them all sit in the back with Paul in the middle—to protect him. After they'd gotten home, they realized he still had the new lunch bucket in his hand and had not let go of it as if it was a treasure he had found. After that they were all more careful who sat where and Paul learned to check the door handles to be sure what he was turning up and down.

We all have had our scraps and bumps in this world. Sometimes they're nasty ones that teach us lessons we didn't want to learn, or that we don't ever want to experience again. Other times, we have to relearn our lessons just to get the message through to us. If we were as smart as we are supposed to be, we would take the lesson learned and store them somewhere in our brains that gives us off a warning signal. Well, guess what? We do have that available to us. Some people believe that the Holy Spirit or the Holy Ghost warns us. Others call it intuition. I prefer the first; but whichever it might be in your case, take time to listen to that still small voice, or that booming loud voice, in your mind that's saying, "Warning, warning, danger ahead." Maybe if we did listen more often, we would be a whole lot better off—and so would this world.

Walter Paul, Jean and Elizabeth Osborn—1944.

The Osborns. Back Row: Walter, Jean and Betty.
Front Row: Elizabeth and Paul—1946.

Walter Paul Osborn, Jr.
Cherry Point Road
Paris, Illinois,
about 1947

The Osborn family.
Back row: Elizabeth and Jean
Front row: Dad Walter, Paul and Mother Elizabeth "Betty"
1947.

# Did Curiosity Kill the Cat?

Have you ever been so curious that it got you in trouble? As a child, my need to know was a thorn in my mother's side. I was always asking questions I had no business asking and got myself into more scrapes because my curiosity got in the way. One time I just couldn't resist asking, "Do cats really have nine lives." Now I never ever hurt a cat. In fact, I love cats, but for some reason, one day I was playing with the kittens and noticed one of the cats had a whisker longer than all the rest. I thought it looked uneven. I went into the house and got my pair of little scissors, grabbed up the kitten and cut back the whisker—just a little too much—so I cut the other whiskers, until that poor kitty had only a few stubs left.

Now a cat's whiskers are their radar, and I had just cut that poor kitten's off. Without their whiskers, cats can't sense a thing at night. It is their unique way of feeling what's out there. They can sense danger, another animal—even humans. I was so sad for that cat. For a long time I carried the cat everywhere so it wouldn't get hurt or lost. Finally, Dad told me it was all right, that the other cats would take care of her.

Boy, was Mom mad at me, and when dad gently explained that they don't grow back. That's why kitten's whiskers are so long at the beginning. Oh, I wanted to glue those whiskers back on.

As for my curiosity, that never really stopped, but after that I was more careful. We all have to be careful of what we're curious about. Kids now days get into way to much trouble with curiosity about drugs, video gaming, and sex way too early—all because someone gets curious.

It also was curiosity that, gave us the airplane, penicillin, lazar surgery, and the double-burger. Maybe, just maybe, a little bit of curiosity is what fuels our creative juices and that in itself is a good thing.

# The Smokehouse

Not too far from my grandparents house sat a little shed, Grandpa Kirkpatrick called the smokehouse. When I was little I thought it was a place where people went to smoke. As I grew up I came to know it's use. I had gone to stay with my grandparents for a short time while Dad and Mom were off to a church convention—when I was a teen. One day, a few weeks after there had been a butchering, Grandpa took my cousin and I into the mysterious building and we found meat and hams hanging up and there was this wonderful smell of hickory and curing meat wafting past our noses. This is where Grandpa Kirkpatrick would also hang all the game he'd hunted. He was quite a good hunter, and he loved it dearly. And Mom told me, that during the depression, they were very grateful he was such a good hunter.

While in that smokehouse we also discovered cracklins— crunching, yet chewy, pieces of pork rind that you could chew on for the longest time and not feel a bit hunger afterwards. After discovering this great treat, we girls would often sneak into the old smokehouse and help ourselves. Unfortunately our moms discovered what we were doing and we both got a fair warning that too much of a good thing could make us sick. They were right. One afternoon we got a bit of a stomach ache and payed for our overindulgent. We regretted every bit of those cracklins we'd stuffed in our mouths. Had we been less greedy, and more careful, we would have enjoyed those wonderful yummy's for a longer time.

As it was, Grandpa put a lock on the door and after that we had to go to him or Grandma to receive our favorite treats.

I realize, now, that we'd gotten hooked on those snacks and we paid a price for it. Sore tummies and a dose of good old Pepto Bizmo—I hated the taste of that stuff—was our just rewards for being greedy.

It seems to me that today we are still like my cousin and me. When we're given something good we tend to be greedy and want more. The more we get, the more we want—and so goes on the vicious circle. Sometimes we need to get off that circle and take good look at ourselves. The old saying: "Money can't buy happiness;" or "You can't get enough of a good thing," are just that—sayings. It's up to us to find what really makes us happy and when we do, life is as good as were those cracklins, if we don't over indulge.

Grandpa Glen and Grandma Nellie Kirkpatrick's house, Bismarck, Illinois.

# Chickens, Eggs and the Rooster

When I was around five years old, Mom and Dad would take me to Grandpa and Grandma Kirkpatrick's to visit. Most of the time, there, I was left alone and I had a habit of sneaking off to the hen house. Many times I could be found in there. I don't remember why, but I would grab the eggs and smash them. Well, that was not a nice thing to do and those eggs were part of my grandparents' paycheck. I guess you could say I was just a little stinker, or maybe I had nothing else to do.

I really had a thing for going out there, and Mom would catch me and scold me, but for some reason I would eventually head back out there. You might say I needed a good spanking. I probably did, and one day when I wasn't paying attention, Grandpa Kirkpatrick followed me out to the hen house. When he saw me destroying those eggs he grabbed me up and put me over his knee and I got the whoppin' of my life. Mom said after that I never went back out to the hen house to destroy eggs just for fun. Instead I went out there to gather them up and work for Grandpa to help him.

Of course my interest in the chickens didn't stop though at the eggs. As I got older I still had it in for the chickens. In my grandfathers chicken yard there were some roosters. One of them was a rather cocky fellow. He would stride around the yard with his Cock-a-doodle-do. He would chase the hens, peck at them and make them mad at him.

I found it amusing to mock him and I got real good at it, too. When I would do my version, he would ruffle his feathers and let out his best cock-a-doodle, and I would just mock him back and swing on the gate. Well, one day Grandma sent me out to gather some eggs. I had, at least, become responsible enough to do that simple job—as Mom put it.

Soon, I took the egg basket and out I went to the hen house. I had just gotten all the eggs gathered into the basket and was on my way back to the gate, when this cocky rooster decided that he had the upper hand. He made a bee line for my legs and he pecked me good. I started to screaming and here came Grandpa.

I was running around the yard trying to keep away from the rooster and he was still chasing me when Grandpa said, "Head for the gate!"

I ran as fast as I could without dropping the basket of eggs. As I got on the other side of the gate that willy old rooster tried to fly up and get me again, but as his wings were clipped he didn't make it.

After looking at my leg and realizing my pride was wounded, he said, "It'll heal, as will everything else. Now maybe you have learned a lesson here. Don't tease the rooster!" Then he said to the rooster on the other side of the fence, "Now as for you rotten bird, I've been waiting for an excuse to get rid of you and now you've given it to me. You will be Sunday dinner." Sure enough that Sunday we all had roasted chicken and noodles.

Well, after that, I had a little more respect for the eggs, chickens, and the roosters, even though they always seemed fairly inept to me. They did provide good food and a means to make some money.

These days, we just go to the grocery store, and buy our eggs. The chickens are already cleaned and sometime even precut for us. I wonder how we would ever get along if we had to gather the eggs, butcher the chickens and cook our own meal from scratch to be able to eat. Life has a way of sending us lessons. In this case the lesson I learned was to be more considerate of animals, particularly roosters that fly and peck. The other lesson is to avoid destroying someone else's property.

## Cows, Milk and Kittens

When I was a youngster, Grandpa Huffman had a good-sized barn. In it were the cows, hay, various tools and cats that lived there. He would milk the cows in the morning, then let them out to feed in the pasture. Letting them feed on the good rich grass made the milk so much better. In the early evening, before supper time, he would herd the cows back into the barn, get them into their stalls and they would feed on hay and grain. It would take him quite awhile to milk the cows, as he didn't have milking machines and the milk was used for their needs as well as being sold locally.

One day while I was there I watched him milk and took a hand at it myself. He had quite a rhythm at that milking. I, on the other hand, didn't do so well—but I tried. This was one place you didn't want to have long finger nails. Cows can be very touchy when it comes to milking and occasionally a cow would get her dander up and kick the bucket or kick Grandpa. They also had a habit of swishing their tails right in your face and many a time those tails has burrs in them and that would really hurt.

On one occasion, a cow decided to be a bit cantankerous and kicked Grandpa and he slapped her on her haunch and told her to quiet down. She didn't seem to get the message, so he got the shackles out and locked her back feet together so she wouldn't kick him again. That sure did the trick and she finally quieted down.

One of the reasons Grandpa Huffman kept cats around in the barn was to be mousers. They would kill the mice and that way the grain wouldn't get bad. For this, the cats would receive rewards. One of those rewards was sitting around near milking time and wait. Their wait was rewarded by a shot of milk in the mouth. I was amazed the first time I saw it. Grandpa Huffman. would sit on his stool, get adjusted and started milking. Ever so

often he would turn a cow's teat in the direction of the cats and squeeze milk right into a cat's mouth. Those cats loved it and he got quite a kick out of it. I thought that was the neatest thing I'd ever seen. I think I remember seeing my dad feed our cats that way once in awhile.

Whether its milk in the mouth, or the rewards of a job well done, those cats were faithful to Grandpa and he loved them for their usefulness.

The same thing applies today. When we do a good job, whether it's cleaning up, doing a good deed for someone or making a yard beautiful, the reward is there for us. Whether it's a hug, money or the good feeling of something accomplished, it's still a reward and it feels so good to receive it.

# A Feisty Little Thing

When I was young, I went to Bible School at Farmer's Chapel Church. We did some fun things, learned stories of the scriptures and at the end there was a program. All the parents were to come and see what we'd done and learned. My parents and I went. The program started, and everything was going well until a little boy put his hand on the back of my pew. I turned around and smacked his hand. Mom scolded me, but when he did it again, I smacked him again, and it became a game for us—but it was disruptive. People behind us chuckled and Mom and Dad were upset with me. I can't say I blame them. Having now gone through similar events with my own children. I think Mom and Dad just wanted me to be a perfect little Miss Sunshine and not get into any trouble. I've always thought "Trouble" should have been my middle name. Besides, there was never anyone else to blame for my mishaps.

To top it off, when it got to be my turn to recite, I got up in front of all those people, and I started off just fine, only to forget the rest of my lines. With some prompting, I got through the piece, but when I got home did I get it from Mom and Dad. I truly sympathize for anyone who has to get up and give a speech. I think that was the day I told myself I would never be afraid to do that again. Later, I found performing in plays really helped me, and someone in a speech class told me to imagine all those people watching were in their underwear, but with clothes as they are today, I nixed that idea. However, I find that if I imagine them in silly hats, it really makes me smile inside. and I feel very at ease getting up and giving a talk in church or almost anywhere. My husband says that unleashed the yak from inside me, because, he says I'm always yakking with someone on the phone or in person. What more can I say? I love to talk!

# Oleo Versus Butter and Pickles to Pickles

There were many a times when I would sneak down to Grandma Kirkpatrick's. There was always something to do, or watch or cook. On such an occasion, while I was at Grandpa and Grandma Kirkpatrick's, she had a whole bunch of cream. On the back porch sat the butter churner. No, it wasn't one of those wooden ones from pioneer days. It was more modern. It had a glass jar base with a lid that screwed on. The lid had a handle that you turned around and around.

Grandma asked if I would like to try my hand at churning. I thought it would be great fun. It was easy at first, but as the cream began to turn to butter it got harder and harder. My arm was hurting a little and by the time I finished they were plum sore, but there, sitting in a pool of liquid buttermilk were lumps of butter. I was so excited.

Grandma put a bit of salt in it and mixed it a little more. Than she put flour-sack material over a bowl and poured the whole thing into it. She brought the four corners together and started to twist the top of the material until it formed a tight ball and all the buttermilk had been squeezed out. She then sat out butter forms and spooned the butter into the forms and carefully smooth them over, put wax paper on them and set them in the refrigerator.

A few years later, when I went to visit, I asked about the butter and she said, "Oh now we can use Oleo." She pulled out this plastic package of white stuff that had a little red dot in the middle. She said, "Now squish it and work it until it turns yellow."

That it was just as much fun as the butter was and a whole lot easier. When I was done squishing, she took it and cut off a corner of it and she kind of squirted it into the butter forms and, like the butter, put the wax paper over it and put it in the refrigerator. Later, when she had baked some fresh bread she brought out both the Oleo and the butter. We taste tested them both and I agreed with her; nothing beats butter!

One of the things I loved to eat on fresh bread was butter and pickles—but not just any pickles. Among the different kinds of pickle grandma made were old-fashioned brine dills, sweet baby gherkins, and my favorite—bread and butter pickles. I loved them so much I could even drink the juice. Now I know it sound plain silly, but there was something in the juice I craved. Mom would catch me drinking vinegar—"vingar," as I called it. She said my body must have had a need for it.

We know today that vinegar is good for the stomach and many other aliments. We also know that the old Oleo was not as good for us, and now we have all of that fancy stuff on the market that is supposed to lower our cholesterol.

Now and then, a little butter, pickles and bread won't hurt us. As in all things, moderation is the key. I try to follow that even though I'm a bit overweight now as the years creep up on me. But I don't think I'll ever give up my pickles, butter, and bread, but I'll do my best in being moderate.

Just as the pickles have a bite to them, we can sometimes have a bite about us, and just like the butter we can be smooth, but when it comes to a good piece of fresh bread we can find ourselves on solid ground, and if we do things with moderation, we can enjoy all the different flavors of our lives.

# The Ol' Rocking Chair

When I was a small child, I would sometimes stay overnight with my grandparents. Since they lived in a small, one-and-a-half bedroom house, many times I'd sleep on the couch and Mother would sleep on a cot in the half bedroom that was really just a curtain drawn to divide off Grandpa and Grandma Kirkpatrick's half—for privacy sake.

One day something new arrived. It was probably one of the first lounge chairs put out by Sears and Roebuck. It didn't lounge back like the ones of today. It was a rocker, but when you pulled a couple of iron rods from the back you could recline it all the way down to a sleeper. It was quite something.

When Grandpa got it put together and showed Grandma, she said, "Land of livin'. Would you ever believe these new fangled chairs." She sat down in it and rocked. Then Grandpa showed us how you could recline it. She just couldn't get over it. She sat down and when he reclined it just a little, she exclaimed," Oh my, one could sleep in it if they wanted to."

"My exact thought," Grandpa told her. "In the daytime it's a chair, but at night our grandchild can sleep on it and she can rock herself until she falls asleep."

Well, as I did just that, it didn't take long for me to fall asleep. It was so much fun for me and it was nearer to the old oil stove so I could keep warmer. I think it was this very chair that when I was sick with a fever, I slept in and got so much better—sooner. At least it seemed so. It was the chair where I climbed onto my grandma's lap and she would read to me. And I would bring all of my dolls and Teddy Bear and put them to sleep in that chair.

It was a sad day, many years later, when the chair finally met it's demise. I almost cried. It held so many memories. I wished I could have kept it. I would've stuck it the corner of a room in my house. It was a piece of my history. Today, though, I make new memories from another lounge chair— my husband's. It's big and dark blue—a man's chair. It's the chair grand- children sit in with him, or they sit in it—two together—when he's not home. It's the chair they fight over to see who gets to sleep in it at night. It's also the chair that our beloved Mindi dog sat in with my husband. I'm not sure we'll ever get rid of that chair because it's Grandpa's big blue chair.

Now I'm sure that most of you have that favorite chair, the one you al- ways sit in. It fits you and no one else. It's your comfort zone. We all like to feel we're keeping in our comfort zone, but just once in a while, step out of it and try something new, just like my grandpa did. You'd be sur- prised just what you might find.

# Stubborn as Stubborn Can Be

Mother always said I had a mind of my own—and that I could be difficult and stubborn. I guess I never saw it that way. I was just always wanting to know how things were done. I would stubbornly ask questions like, "How do you milk a cow? How are kittens born? How come I couldn't have lots of curls just like Shirley Temple?" And therein laid a real problem.

Valerie Huffman—1948.

At about eleven or twelve, I had beautiful wavy hair. I really didn't need to curl it, but I got it into my head that if I got a perm I could have those wonderful curls like all the other little girls were wearing. I most likely begged, pleaded and boo-hooed until my mom gave in and told me I could get a perm. Well, perms in the late 1940s weren't what they are today. Not only did they stink to high heavens, but they were so harsh on the hair that if you left them on just a little too long you could do real damage to your hair and scalp.

I do think it was a home perm that I got, and I think things went wrong within the first few minutes, because it not only stank, but it burned my scalp, and by the time we'd waited the time it said to wait, my hair was beyond help. I looked like I'd stuck my finger in a light socket. My hair was a frizzy mess. It was so bad we could barely get a comb through it. We finally had to cut it off—just when it was time to make an appointment to have my picture taken for school.

I was so mortified at having that picture in the school book that when the pictures came back I refused to hand any of them out. Suffice to say, I still have one of those awful pictures and yes, my hair still looks as if lighting had struck me.

Sometimes it can be alright to be stubborn, like when someone tries to talk you into something that's wrong—and you know it. Then you can be stubborn and say, "No." You can be stubborn when you know, down-deep inside, that you're right about something and you feel good about it. Being stubborn can be used to do good as long as it's harnessed, just like a mule, and as the old saying goes, "You can push a mule only so far and then he will sit down on you." So the next time you get that stubborn feeling, just ask yourself, "Do I want to feel good or do I want to feel like a mule." I find I'd rather feel good about me.

Here I am at twelve,
with my super curly hair.

Dad Glenn Huffman and me.

# From Farm to Parish

Dad's first official ministry, Locust Grove United Brethern Church—1954.

When I was about twelve, my dad, who'd been a farmer and had farmed land with my grandfather, decided to answer the call to become a minister. It was a hard decision because it meant uprooting Mother and me from all the family, friends and community we had loved. I'm not sure Mom was to happy about it, but in those days a wife went where her husband went. As the Bible says in the *Old Testament*, "You shall leave your father and mother and cleave unto your husband, and he to you, and you shall become one."

As for me, I was just there because I had to be. I wasn't a happy camper about it. As a matter of fact, I hated every bit of the move, and being the outsider when we got there really didn't help any. I soon found out that being the PK (preacher's kid) was looked down upon. I was made fun of, and not too many of the kids in the church where Dad first started out would have anything to do with me. There was one girl, though, that befriended me. She was handicapped because of polio. Together we made life bearable my first year there.

When we moved into the parsonage, we found it to be old, and had no bathroom and no workable kitchen. It should have had running water as it had an old pump in the big kitchen sink that must have been used to wash clothes. I remember Mom saying, "There had better be running water in here soon—and a bathroom."

We did have a wall phone, but when you picked up to call, you would hear other phones being picked up. We were on a party line. Boy, have we come a long way with our cell phones, tweeting and texting. Could you imagine what it would be like with just a wall phone?

Since dad wasn't a full-fledged minister and was going to college on the side, we were payed $750 for the first six months from the Locust Grove Church. To supplement, we grew our own garden to make ends meet. We had our own chickens for eggs and food. Sometimes, we would get stuff from the people in the church. One time a goose was brought to us. It was old and so greasy we could hardly eat it. It ended up as soup as Mom let nothing go to waste. In the summer we grew veggies in the garden and Mom and Dad had planted lots of peas. That was a bumper year and I can still remember telling Mom how much I hated hulling all those peas and that I never wanted to see another pea in my whole life. Her reply was, "You may say that now, but when winter comes and you are hungry, you will be glad we processed those peas."

You know what? She was right! On a cold winter night sitting down to bowl of peas cooked with a few potatoes in them was really quite yummy. Sometimes she would even put a little cream in with them.

One of the responsibilities of the pastor, of course, was to preach on Sunday, see to the needs of the sick, perform marriages, funerals, and oddly enough, at this small church, he also cut the grass, trimmed around the headstones and cleaned the church each week.

When I was thirteen, I ended up with the mumps. I can honestly say nothing is more miserable than having your cheeks swollen and looking like a chipmunk that stuffed himself only to realize he had too much in his cheeks and then couldn't unload them.

Not only did I get them, but my dad, (Grandma had assured my mom that he'd had them when he was a boy), came down with a good case of them on both sides. Now, it was even more miserable for him than for me. There was no one to preach that Sunday, so my mom got it together and *she* preached a darn good sermon. We all survived the event and now laugh about it as our "Chipmunk" days. It's experiences like this that helps us grow and become more appreciative of what we have now. And yes, I still like peas!

The Wood River Parish for the third church where Dad preached.

## Sunburns and Skunks

Have you ever wished something so bad that you'd suffer the pains of getting it?

When I was about sixteen, Mom and Dad took my foster sister, Bonnie and I to Horse Shoe Bend, Missouri. We were elated that we would be able to go to a place where we could get a summer tan—away from all the rest of the kids we knew. This was a big thing for us. It would be compared now to going to Daytona Beach, Florida, or to a great beach in California.

In the late 1950s, Horse Shoe Bend was the place to be as a vacation spot for us. We packed and got into Dad's '56 Chevy and off we went on a great adventure of sun, water and hmm—maybe the chance to meet a cute boy or two. Little did we know that there things weren't going to go as we'd planned.

We arrived early in the evening. We had rented a cabin and Bonnie and I got settled in our room. It had a set of bunk beds, a dresser and a night table. That was about it. We were a little disappointed it wasn't a little fancier, but still we were there and we were looking forward to a great time the next day.

The following morning we woke up to sunshine and a good breakfast Mom had fixed, then we all took off for some sight-seeing. We took in all the wonderful crafts and little stores the area offered, and then came back to the cabin for lunch.

After lunch Bonnie and I changed our clothes and headed for the beach. We gathered all of our stuff: big towels, suntan lotion, sunglasses, books to read, something to drink and off we went with great anticipation.

When we got to the beach, got set up and started to enjoy the afternoon, we lathered ourselves with suntan lotion and tried to look good in case a cute boy or two came along.

Well, there were some people on the beach, but none of them were young and cute. Little kids ran by and threw sand at us and after a while we turned ourselves over for a little more tanning on the other side.

Mom came down and told us not to stay out to long and we said we wouldn't and that we planned getting into the water, too. She left us to go rest and would later fix some supper. We were laying there talking and soon we both fell asleep in the warm sun.

When we woke up, it was much later in the afternoon. Our backs were a little red and by the time we got to the cabin our backs looked like two red lobsters that had been cooked too long. Oh, the agony of it all. Oh, the humiliation of it as we walked passed two cute guys and couldn't bear to smile at them because we hurt to much.

Of course, when we got back we got a royal tongue lashing by Mom for staying out to long. She told us to take cold showers and then she had us pat each others backs dry. Then she sprinkled vinegar all over our backs. Oh did that ever sting, just as much as the tongue lashing we'd gotten—and it didn't stop there. As miserable as we were our misery had only begun.

Later that night, after another application of vinegar and a little burn cream, we tried to settle in for a night's sleep. That was not to be. We were so sore, we couldn't stand to have the sheets over us. To top that off, there were polecats in the area. Now a polecat is sometimes called a skunk and they come in varieties of patterns in colors of black, brown and white. Most of the ones we see are the stripped kind. However, down there in the Ozarks they had the spotted ones.

Well, we were laying there and I looked out the window, which happened to be at ground level, and saw this good-sized creature go by. With him came an aroma I can only explain as putrid and sicking. He didn't seem to want to leave our area and we hollowed out for my dad to come.

He came downstairs and said, "Yup, that's a skunk for sure," and then just chuckled at our dilemma. "It'll go away soon. It's looking for food."

Oh the misery of that night. Our vacation was ruined as far as we were concerned.

The next day it rained and we were stuck inside. Just was well. We were in no mood to go anywhere. We played board games with Mom and Dad and talked about the boys we would liked to have seen at the beach and the ones we did see, but alas, too late. We ended the day by going out for our meal.

On day four, it was lovely out and we did go to the beach and enjoyed a limited time, there. And we saw some cute guys, but they never noticed us. We were so disappointed, and the whole trip, as far as we were concerned, was a bust. Mom and Dad thought it was wonderful. They had gotten lots of rest. Dad had gotten to go fishing, and that night we enjoyed a good fish dinner. We packed up the last day and took one more look around and then left for home.

As for getting what we wanted: we did get suntans and were able to boast of them after we had peeled for a few days. As for saying we'd met any cute boys, we may have exaggerated a bit, but hey, we had to look good with our friends. We also learned a valuable lesson. Be careful what you wish for. It can sometimes backfire on you and you're left with memories you'd just as soon forget. You know, I'd swear I can still smell that polecat sometimes when the wind is just right.

A teenageer at last.

Leaving high school—1959.

Valerie Huffman's
high school graduation photo—1959.

## Marriage and Cowboy Boots

During the time I was a teenager, Dad was a minister. He had a little church in Paris, Illinois. One of his duties was to perform marriages. Sometimes they would be planned and were lovely, and sometimes people would just call him up and want to get married that very day. On one such occasion, a couple called dad and wanted to get married that evening. Most of the time, Mom and I were witnesses, but this time I was to go on a date and the couple wanted Mom to play some music.

When they arrived I was about to leave on my date with a young man I'll call Bill. Now Bill, as usual, wore a cowboy hat, shirt and cowboy boots, and I was wearing jeans and a blouse. Well, Dad asked us to witness the wedding, and there wasn't time for him to go home and change, and we were due at a get-together with friends for a hay ride.

We couldn't say no to Dad, and the couple didn't seem to mind that we were in cowboy attire, but if we weren't a sight standing there while Mom played some appropriate music for a wedding. I do think it made Bill a bit nervous. As for me, I thought it was cool to be a part of someone starting their lives together. However, after we left for our hayride I found that Bill was a bit sullen and he didn't pay much attention to me. It made me a bit mad at him and we kind of parted our ways.

I had a friend, Katy. She and another friend, Sue, ended up going on a double date with Katy, and her boy friend. He had his cousin in the car and Sue ended up sitting with him in the front seat—since he was driving.

On the way home from the hayride he pulled over and said he wanted to talk with her. She thought he was cute and so they ended up pulling over on the side of the country road they were on. Soon talk started to become something else and Sue called him on it. After all she hardly knew him. He tried to apologize to her. Well, his way of apologizing wasn't the way she thought a young woman should be apologized to and his advances to her weren't very honorable. To say the least, she was really miffed at him and they got into a bit of a fight and Sue finally said, "Be that way, I sure wouldn't want *this* for a boyfriend!"

He tried to stop her, but she countered, "Leave me along. I'll just walk home if you don't mind."

Well, the couple in the back of the car were astonished, and before they all knew it, Sue had gotten out of the car and had started walking home, alone, in the dark.

Katy said, "I'm with you," and she climbed out, too. The girls walked along the country road with only the moon shining down on them.

Within a few minutes here came the boys in the car, driving up slowly alongside them.

"Hey we're sorry," they said. "Now get back into the car."

"No, we're not girls you can brag about to the other boys. We won't be treated like that, so get used to it!"

"All right! We're really sorry. Please get in the car and let us take you home. If anything happened to either of you, we'd be to blame. We sure don't want your folks to get mad at us!"

"You promise? No more monkey business?" they asked.

"Scouts honor," they replied.

"Well, What do you think, Katy?" Sue asked.

"Hmm, I think they've learned their lesson."

They got back in the car and Sue sat all the way over by the door—as did Katy.

Shortly after the incident, they all split up and went their separate ways, and Katy and Sue sure did let the other girls know those two boys had octopus arms and couldn't keep them to themselves.

As for Bill, I never did date him again, but kept my cowboy boots as a memory of a lesson well learned. As for the couple that got married, they had a happily-ever-after-life and God blessed them for it. As for me. I went on to meet the man of my dreams, but that's another story.

# The Prom Dress

Not too long ago, my mother gave me something that really brought back the memories of my high-school life. It was my orchid prom dress. It wasn't the first one, but it was my first one that had been purchased.

Because we were not exactly rolling in money, and Pastors, in those days, earned very little, my first prom dress was made by Mom. In fact, most of the clothing I wore was made by Mother, who was an excellent seamstress. She made some of the nicest clothing anyone would want to wear. However, I was sometimes made fun of because of my homemade clothes. It made me even more insecure than I already was.

My first Prom almost didn't happen. I was sixteen and was not allowed to date. I could go in groups, but Mom and Dad felt that waiting until I was seventeen was more appropriate. As it happened, though, a young man who'd graduated early and was a member of the church where Dad preached, came to us and asked if he could have the pleasure of escorting me to the dance—more of a chaperone than a date. As he was going into the military soon, and had been a good friend to us all, Mom felt he would be safe to be with, and I could then mingle with some of my peers without being embarrassed that I had no date. The dress she made was lovely and was admired by a few of my friends. It was a fun night and I really wished it wouldn't end. However, when that last dance was announced, the young man escorting me came over and ask me to dance. That was the highlight of my night. I felt just like Cinderella who had found her prince.

A couple of weeks later, I received a letter in the mail from this young man telling me of his enrollment in the military. We wrote off and on for a while, and then I got a letter that rocked my world. With the letter came the break-up of our friendship. He'd found the girl of his dreams and they were to be married. A few tears later, and a couple of honks on a tissue, I told Mom and Dad. They were happy for him, and in my own way, I knew I was, too.

Two years later we moved from Moweaqua to Paris. The day we moved, it was raining cats and dogs and lightning and thunder rolled through the sky. It was dark and dreary, and my first opinion of the place was that I was not going to like it one bit. After a few days of getting settled into another old house, I met Katy. She was bright, and well to do and took one look at me and said, "We need to do a make over on you." She showed me what to wear and how to wear it—matching my colors so I would fit in better with the class of kids at the school I'd be attending. In those days there were the upper crusts, the mediums and the scaggs.

Besides her, I met Bonnita. She was a beautiful girl with long, light-brown hair and a beautiful complexion that looked like she was always wearing rouge. She and I got to be great friends—and still are. Due to family circumstances, she came to live with us as a foster child and for the first time I had a sister. I'm sure we girls gave my folks a run for their money.

In my junior year, I wore the same dress Mom had made for the previous year's prom. No one thought anything of it because it was new to them. Time went on and Bonnita and I both had boyfriends.

When our senior year arrived, Mother approached me and asked about making a prom dress for me. I told her I wanted a store-bought dress like the other girls. She said, "That costs money," but I was insistent on it, and so the money was found and we went shopping. Oh I know, a dress made by her would have been lovely, but I was determined to fit in and have that special dress. I guess I might have been a bit of a brat—as she has reminded me through the years. Well, we found one that we both agreed looked good on me and bought it. I was so proud of that dress. She told me it would be the only one she would buy for the year, and I would have to wear it to the Prom *and* the Spring Fling, too.

The time came when both Bonnita and I were all dressed up in our lovely dresses and Dad took pictures. I was so proud of my dress and off we went to the Prom feeling like princesses. We had a wonderful time and when Spring Fling came for graduation, I again wore the same dress with a beautiful Gardenia pinned to the front and a set of stiff crinolines that made it flair out at the bottom. It looked like a different dress. After school was out, the dress was carefully cleaned and put away in a plastic bag never to be seen again until the day a few years ago. Mom gave it to me.

I knew I couldn't get into it. Over fifty some odd years later, I'd gained a lot of weight. I thought to myself, *what will I do with this*. I hung it in my closet for a long time until a friend's daughter came over one day and we got to talking. She said she wished she could get hold of an old '50s dress, poodle skirt or something from that era. A light went off in my head, and I soon came back with the prom dress in hand. She took one look at it and said, "This is perfect for me to wear to the '50s dance at church!" It was such a joy for me to see that dress back in use. It had made someone else as happy as it had made me.

Now the dress hangs back in my closet. Perhaps it will become useful again before it falls apart. It's strange how we take such pride in such simple things. Looking a certain way is so important to a girl when she's young, but now, years later, I realize any dress would have done. It was the company that was important. Perhaps we all have that prom dress, old jacket, or hat we can't give up. Why should we? We need to enjoy those treasures. Live today. Tomorrow is yet to come.

# A Rare Treasure

We celebrated our 50th Wedding Anniversary in 2010. As we reflected back I thought of the first day I met my husband.

It was a Friday and I was sitting at the counter at the local diner located inside a Woolworth store. Betty, the woman who ran the diner, was always friendly and always asked how we girls, who would take a break from the upstairs Hairdressers College, were doing. And she would occasionally slip us a free coke or lemonade.

On this particular day she was especially cheerful. She came over to us and said our drinks were on the house.

"Hey what's got you so cheery today?" I asked her.

My friend next to me almost echoed my question.

"Oh," Betty said with a grin that lit up her face, "our son is home from Germany."

"Germany? That's really neat, Betty. I'm glad you have him back," I said.

"Oops. Got a customer. Talk with you later, Oh, by the way, I'd like you to meet him."

"Sure Betty, just name the time. I'd love to meet the guy you're always talking about." Then she hurried to the waiting customer.

"Are you crazy?" my friend asked me. "What if he's a total flake?"

"Nothing could be worse than what I've just got done dating. He was one of the worse guys I've ever dated, and I hope I never have to deal with him again," I said, thinking back to my previous summer.

About that time a very handsome young man walked into the diner and sat down at the end of the counter. He was wearing an Army uniform, and all I could say to my friend was a big, "WOW!"

"Wow, and how!" She echoed.

"Where in the world did he from? I've never seen him here before," I chirped.

"Oh, come to mama," she said in a catty manner. "Down girl. Hold on to your hat."

"He's probably got a girl already waiting for him," I replied with a sigh.

We watched as Betty waited on the guy at the end of the counter that we were drooling over. He drank a coke and in a few minutes he was gone. We figured we'd never to see again. We were just finishing our sandwiches when Betty walked over to us. "Val, I really do want you to meet my son."

"O.K. Fine. Whenever. We've got to get back upstairs. Our lunch break's over.

"How about this afternoon after you get off? Just sit down at counter, on the stool next to the end, and I'll have him come by."

"Fine with me, Betty. We've got to run. You know how the hair coach gets of we're late. See you this afternoon."

"Yes, yes. Okay!" she said as she waved us off.

We ran back upstairs just in time to see the proprietor of the Hair college looking down her nose at us through her old-fashioned wire glasses.

"Twelve thirty? You two are five minutes late," she said impatiently.

Those next two hours dragged. I was so nervous I almost burnt a woman's hair with the curling iron. As I got through the final set, the teacher said to us, "OK, girls you'll be having a test tomorrow, so study, study, study."

As 2:30 p.m. approached, we were allowed to do each other's hair for the weekend. I told my friend, "Let's get this done so I can get down there on time. I don't know what to expect, but I sure do want to look good, at least."

She agreed. By 3:15 p.m. we were looking good.

"Well, I'll see you tomorrow," I said.

"Oh, no you won't! I'm going with you. Do you think I'm going to miss a chance at seeing what this guy looks like that you're supposed to meet? Not on the hair of your head—that I just did."

So off we went down the stairs, into the Woolworth store and straight to the counter.

"Hi, Betty," we chimed together—like two peas in a pod.

"What's your pleasure, girls?" she asked.

"Two cherry cokes, please?" I said.

She brought them and we settled in, but not for long. Out of the corner of my eye I saw the same guy we'd seen earlier in the Army uniform. This time he had civvies on. He was just as cute and handsome without the uniform. He came and sat down by me. *Hmm,* I thought, *if only*—

He ordered a cup of Joe, and as he poured the cream into it, I could see he was a little nervous.

About that time Betty leaned over the counter and said, "Val, I'd like you to meet my son, Walter Paul Osborn. Son, this is Valerie Huffman."

I couldn't believe it! Here I was sitting beside the very guy my friend and I had ogled earlier. Shelly nudged me and said in a whisper, "It's him."

"I know, I know. Would you please keep it down a bit. He'll hear you and think we're a couple of dodo's."

Walter cleared his throat and said, in a bit of a shaky voice, "Glad to meet you."

"Oh, the same here. Your Mom told us you were coming home, and she said you'd been in the military."

"Yeah, I just got out," he replied, and then picked up his cup of coffee which clinked against the saucer.

We sat there looking at each other and I just knew I'd found one of those hidden treasures people talk about.

Shelly could see it too, and she blurted out, "O.K., kiddo. It's been nice, but I've gotta run. I've got a test tomorrow to study for. See ya."

She was out the door before I could say, "I need a ride."

We sat there for a while, just talking with Betty about things. I don't even remember what things. All I could think about was how cute this guy was. Then a thought suddenly hit me. "Oh gosh, I've got a test, too. Oh Geez, would you look at the time, I've got to run, too. It was nice meeting you, Walter." I looked out the front window of the store. It had started to rain.

Oh man, I just got my hair done and it was raining. Shelly had taken off on me, and Dad was at the hospital visiting the sick. "I don't even have an umbrella," I murmured.

Betty spoke up, "Can Walter take you home?"

"Huh? Oh sure," he said with a cough. I though he was going to choke on those words. Then he got up and helped me with my books and ushered me to his car. It was a '56 Chevy—blue and white—similar to Dad's car.

We drove home in just a few minutes. There wasn't much talking except, "Where do you live?" and "How long have you lived here?"

When we got to my house, he pulled up to the curb, turned off the engine and ask me, rather carefully, "Would you like to go out tonight?"

Oh, how I wanted to say yes, but because of the test the next day, I knew Mother would have a cat fit if I went out. So I said, "I'd love to go, but I have a test tomorrow and I've got to study."

He looked disappointed, and I thought, *Oh Val, you've done it now.* I followed up by saying, "However if you're free tomorrow night, maybe we could go to a movie."

"Sure that would be great!" he said with a smile.

I told him to be there about six o'clock, and I started to grab up my books to get out of the car, but he was out the door and around to my side before I could say jumpin' jehoshaphat. He carried them to the porch and said, "I'll see you tomorrow."

"Great. See you then. About 6:00 p.m.?" I added and went inside.

The next day I passed my test with flying colors and that's what I did on the way home—fly. I had a date to get ready for. That evening Walter came up to the door, rang the doorbell and Dad answered it.

"Hello sir, I'm Walter Osborn, I've come to pick up your daughter for our date."

They exchanged a few pleasantries and soon we left. As luck would have it, the only movie theater that was showing the movie we wanted to see was in Danville, so we headed that way. We enjoyed the movie, and on the way back, Lady Luck struck us again. We got a real flat tire!

In the 1950s there were no cell phones and almost everything was closed. Walter fixed the tire and we beat it home. When we got there he asked what I was doing on Sunday. I told him I went to church, and I asked him if he wanted to go with me.

"Yes," he answered.

The next day he showed up right on time. After church he said he had to be with his family. They were having a dinner for his return and could he see me the next weekend because he'd just gotten a job in Attica, Indiana.

I said, "Of course." After that we saw each other every weekend. And on Wednesday nights he would call me.

After a few months of dating, we decided that calling him Walter or Jr. just didn't fit him, so he started to go by his middle name—Paul. Then one day, he came to my father and asked for my hand in marriage and *then* popped the question to me. I didn't have to think long. "Yes, I'd love to."

My mother told me she just had a feeling this was to be the man for me. She told us to give her at least six months to make the dress and prepare everything for the wedding. It was a whirlwind of a time. Not only was I getting married, but had to take my State Finals from Hairdressing Academy. Dad and Mom took me to Chicago for my test, and I was so nervous, I passed with flying colors. We then focused on the wedding. The dress Mom made me looked like it came from a bridal book. It had a satin underdress and an overdress of Chantilly lace. I felt I looked like a picture on the cover of a bridal book.

Since Dad, being the minister of our church, was to perform the wedding, he couldn't give me away. We had to find someone else. If we chose either grandparent, or any of the uncles, then we would have a family feud. Then an idea came to me. Why not ask my only male cousin—Lloyd. Most people called him Doc, and I just knew he was the answer to our dilemma. He laughed and said he would do it.

Doc had red hair and a red beard. I wasn't happy about that beard and I mentioned to him that it would look really good if he were to shave it off.

He laughed and said, "Oh no, I've got to keep it on. Why how would I look without it?

His wife of that time said, "A heck of a lot better." Then she said to me, very quietly, "Don't worry, I'll see that its gone by morning light."

I nodded and thought to myself, *She'll get the job done.*

I found out, later, that she had attempted to shave it off while he slept and he woke up. At that point, he told he'd never had any idea of keeping it.

The wedding came off without a hitch. Paul was so handsome in his black suit and my dress looked great. The walk down the isle of the church was kind of silly as I was so short, even in my glass high heels and Doc towered over me with his red hair. I almost stepped on my dress at one point and came darn near throwing us off step. However, we made it and so have Paul and I—all these years. I still have that dress and I dream of a granddaughter, or a great grandchild, wanting to wear it. I'm not holding my breath on that, though.

Fifteen years later—in 1975—we went on a family trip to Washington, D.C. with our two children and renewed our vows, there, in a sacred ceremony in the temple of the Lord. We were sealed together for time and all eternity. There are, in our lives, such times that stand out, and I found such a rare treasure in my husband. I wouldn't change that treasure for all the gold in the world.

I look back and realize how the Lord works in mysterious ways and how hidden treasure can be a rain shower away. Because of that wonderful mother of Paul's, I found a companion for this life and for the eternities. Sometimes we overlook those things, and people that can otherwise enrich our lives.

Our 1960 Hairdressing Academy class.
I am seated on the first row at far right.

# F. W. Woolworth Co.

BACON and TOMATO . . . . . . . . . . . .50c
*Toasted Three Decker Sandwich*
BAKED HAM and CHEESE . . . . . . . .60c
*Toasted Three Decker Sandwich*
CHICKEN SALAD . . . . . . . . . . . . . . . .65c
*Toasted Three Decker Sandwich*
HAM SALAD and EGG SALAD . . . . .50c
*Toasted Three Decker Sandwich*
*Above available on two slices of bread on request.*

### PLAIN or TOASTED SANDWICHES

HAM SALAD Sandwich . . . . . . . . . . .30c

EGG SALAD Sandwich . . . . . . . . . . .30c

AMERICAN CHEESE Sandwich . . . . . .30c

PRESSED HAM Sandwich . . . . . . . . . .30c

### FOR A REAL TREAT!
TRY OUR SUPER DE-LUXE HAM SANDWICH - BAKED HAM SLICED VERY THIN AND STACKED
HIGH ON PLAIN BREAD, TOAST OR HARD ROLL
40¢  YOU WILL LIKE IT!  40¢

## Fountain Features

| DE LUXE | SUPER JUMBO | EXTRA RICH |
| TULIP SUNDAE 25c | BANANA SPLIT 39c | ICE CREAM SODA 25c |

DE LUXE — TULIP SUNDAE 25c
2 Dippers of Ice Cream covered with Crushed Fruit or Fresh Fruits in Season
CHOICE OF
STRAWBERRY, PINEAPPLE, CHERRY, CHOCOLATE OR HOT FUDGE
Topped with Whipped Topping Roasted Nuts and Cherry Ring

SUPER JUMBO — BANANA SPLIT 39c
½ Banana covered with 3 Dippers of Ice Cream and Crushed Fruits or Fresh Fruits in Season
CHOICE OF
STRAWBERRY, PINEAPPLE, CHERRY, CHOCOLATE OR HOT FUDGE
Topped with Whipped Topping and Roasted Nuts

EXTRA RICH — ICE CREAM SODA 25c
POPULAR FLAVORS
Made with 2 Dippers of Ice Cream Crushed Fruit or Fresh Fruits In Season

MALTED MILK . . . . . . . . . . . . . . . . . . . . . . . . . . . . . . . .25c
*Popular FLAVORS      Made with 2 Dippers of Ice Cream*
MILK SHAKE . . . . . . . . . . . . . . . . . . . . . . . . . . . . . . . . .25c
*Popular FLAVORS      Made with 2 Dippers of Ice Cream*
BANANA SPLIT *Regular* . . . . . . . . . . . . . . . . . . . . . . .25c
*Popular FLAVORS      Made with 3 Dippers of Ice Cream*
FRESH ORANGE JUICE . . . . . . . . . *Regular* 20c  Large  30c
*Freshly Squeezed to Order*

HOT NESTLE'S WITH WHIPPED TOPPING . . . . .15c
AND WAFERS

## Home Style Desserts

APPLE PIE . . . . . . . . . . . . . . . . . Per Cut 15c
*10¢ Additional with Ice Cream*
LAYER CAKE . . . . . . . . . . . . . . . . . Per Cut 15c
*10¢ Additional with Ice Cream*

### WOOLWORTH COFFEE — ALWAYS GOOD

A Lunch counter Menu at the time Paul and I met.

Walter Paul Osborn in uniform.
He served in Germany from 1956-1959.

On my Wedding Day, being "given away"
by my only male cousin, Lloyd "Doc" Cunningham, April 10, 1960.

Valerie and Walter Paul Osborn on our Wedding Day,
April 10, 1960, E.U.B. Church—Paris, Illinois.

# A Special Present

About ten months after Paul and I were married, we decided to start a family. We were young and strong, and felt we were both ready for that step. After a bit of time passed, I had the pleasure of informing him we were pregnant.

When Mom heard the news she was right on the ball, making her first baby quilt.

The baby was due at the end of November. Shortly before this had happened we had moved from Paris to Champaign—where we built our first home. We were worried that they wouldn't finish the house in time and we really needed to be in our new home before the baby arrived. Fortunately they took our pleading to heart and in the early Fall we moved into our new home.

When the time neared, I went into labor toward the end of the month. Although my pains were there, the doctor felt the baby was too small, so I was given a shot to stop possible labor pains and sent home. For the next three weeks I had stomach pains. Sometimes they were strong and sometimes they settled down and I was fine, but I was beginning to get worried, and so was the doctor, as the pain persisted on being a part of my life. He realized that maybe I had indeed been in the first stages of labor back when they first started. By the time December 20th came around, the doctor said, "If you don't go into full labor before Christmas, we'll go ahead and induce it further." I thought that doctor was crazy, and I wasn't a happy mommy-to-be.

On the evening of December 21st, my labor pains finally exploded into one continuing pain, and we rushed to the hospital. The pain was so bad, they gave me shots in my back and a drip that knocked me out. I don't remember much about the birth, only that they told me to push and I did. The next thing I knew, we had a baby girl.

I finally got to see her when I woke up. She was like a little angel. Her hair was so long the nurses had put bows in it, and her finger nails and eye lashes were so long the nails had curled under. Of course, they cut them back.

The doctor did admit that perhaps he may have misjudged the estimated date of delivery and that as developed as she was, she could have come earlier. The birth wasn't easy for me as I was small and young and the Doctor had to cut me to allow her to be born. I sometimes wonder if the medications I was given, and the trauma of the birth, played a part in her developing health problems.

I wanted was to go home before Christmas. In those days they made mothers stay in the hospital longer, unlike today when you have the baby they throw you out on the street. That's advanced medicine for you!

I asked the doctor about getting out before Christmas. He said no. I said I wanted to home Christmas Day. He finally saw that I wasn't going to give up, so he told me that if I could walk down the hallway and back, I could go home. Now this was not an easy feat as I had stitches and was very sore, but I was determined, and so after soaking in a sitz baths of warm water, I dressed myself, and with some help from Paul and I grabbed hold of the railing and walked the length of the hallway.

On Christmas Day we brought our little angel home. Mom and Dad had Christmas dinner waiting for us. So was a special pillow called a donut as that was the only way I could sit down! But it was one of the most wonderful Christmases I've had—apart from having one with my five grandchildren.

Christmas presents come in all sizes and package and the little bundle we were given was so very special. We knew that from the beginning, when we first held our precious Donna.

When Donna was just about three, I was pregnant with our second child. We were on our way to see the doctor and had just gotten into an elevator. It was winter and Donna was dressed in a beautiful red coat and bonnet with white furry trimming. She looked like a miniature Shirley Temple in a movie I'd once seen. An elderly gentleman got on to the elevator with us. We were standing there, waiting for the elevator to arrive at our floor.

The stranger leaned over. "My, what a pretty little girl you are."

She replied, "I'm not suppose to talk to stwrangers," in a firm tone.

"Well, my goodness, we wouldn't want you to do that would we?" he said with a chuckle. Then he introduced himself to her properly. "Now that we've been introduced, is it all right if I say what a lovely coat you have on?"

Without a pause, she replied, "My grandma made it for me." Then she curtsied and said a nice thank you. By that time the elevator had reached our floor and we said goodbye.

We never saw the man again, but I was impressed with my daughter. We had told her she should always tell us if anyone tried to speak to her that she didn't know, and she followed our instruction to the T. This was in the 1960s when people were just beginning to be more afraid. The Vietnam War was still going on, and during war time nothing seems the same.

Shortly after this incident, our daughter came down with a rare blood disorder, and I thought my world of a loving husband, a baby on the way and my sweet angel girl was going to crash and burn around me.

As fate or a higher power would have it—I want to think it was God's hand in this—help came to us. We had a very good pediatrician who saw the signs of this disorder and took quick action. With a new medicine flown in from Children's hospital, and iron supplements, our little girl slowly gained her strength back. Soon after, in the spring of 1965, we had a healthy baby boy.

Through the years, our daughter has faced some overwhelming health problems. She had Endometriosis so bad that a complete hysterectomy was needed, which left her unable to have children.

Later on, she was found to have a Congenital condition called Chiari Malformation which then caused Syringomyelia. Later, a serious car accident exacerbated her condition and left her with permanent spinal-cord damage. Surgery was needed to correct the Chiari Malformation so further damage would not occur. Through all of this, she has remained a strong-willed, faithful woman to her beliefs.

Before the spinal injury, she found a wonderful man to share the rest of her life with. Although Owen Hemmert, too, had been in an accident which left him a paraplegic, he is a strong man. He worked himself back into life with little therapy and a will to survive after his first marriage fell apart and he was left to fend for himself.

Fortunately Owen's mother and father helped him, and had faith in his abilities to survive. He worked for the Railroad and was able to move to a different state—giving him a chance at a new life. He is talented—and full of life. We love him like a second son. Although he and Donna had both been previously married, they have been able to come together in one common bond of love and devotion to each other. They love everyone else's children like their own, and they take wonderful care of their three cats—Bobbi Cat, Kara Cat and Miss Dot.

Now I know some of you have either had a baby, or been there for a birth of a grandchild, niece or nephew. They are all such special gifts—given to us to take care of and nurture so they can grow up to be wonderful adults. There will never be a present as precious as the birth of our special child—our daughter. And no gift as wonderful as a gift of the heart as the following below expresses.

Little Donna Osborn.

## Gifts Of The Heart

Some gifts are given because they are expected
Some gift are given to honor the respected
Others are given because you have to
Some are given just because it's
Something you want to do
But the sweetest gifts of those that come to you
Because they have come from that part
of the soul of someone so dear
that they come straight from the heart

One of Donna's
cross-stitched pictures.

WHEN YOU
MEET A PERSON
WITHOUT A SMILE
GIVE HIM
ONE OF YOURS

Me with Mildred, little Donna and Grandpa Glen Kirkpatrick—1962.

Me with Mildred, Donna and Grandma Nellie Kirkpatrick—1962.
A four-generation photo.

Donna and Owen Hemmert on their Wedding Day,
San Diego, California—May 1, 2001.

# Chili, Wagon, Bugs and Lots of Love

In 1965, just as our daughter was getting better from her illness, I was pregnant with our son. It seemed, with him, I had all kinds of craving, while with Donna I was usually having morning sickness right into my 7<sup>th</sup> month. With Mike I could eat just about anything I wanted, and that was a problem. We lived in Bloomington, Illinois, and not too far from us sat the original Steak n' Shake restaurant. They serve hamburger and the best chili I've had ever had. Every time we'd go near the place, my craving would rear its ugly head and I would make Paul stop for at least a cup of it. It got to be so bad Paul would purposely go another way to avoid that place.

One late afternoon, when we had gone to the doctor for a checkup on me and our baby, he forgot about my craving and drove near the restaurant. My craving was so strong, I begged him to stop. So we did, and I ate that chili with great pleasure. Later that evening, though, I started having what I thought was a bad stomach ache. Oh I knew I shouldn't have eaten a whole bowl of chili. My stomach got more upset and I went to the bathroom. The cramps in my abdomen became stronger and soon I had the urge to urinate. As I did, water gushed of me and when I checked, I was bleeding. Now you might say, "Didn't she know she was in labor?"

No! Mike wasn't due for more than two weeks and I had no idea he was going to come so soon. After all, the doctor had told us we had plenty of time.

After I'd discovered I was bleeding, I woke Paul and we headed for the hospital. When we got there we were put into a pre-birthing room and within a little time I was ready to give birth. I had decided to have a natural birth because, with the Donna, I'd had no idea what was going on.

Within in an hour I had disposed of my chili, and told the nurses the baby was coming. The nurses said that couldn't be. I wasn't fully dilated, but fully or not, I had such a strong urge to push and they couldn't stop me. They took me straight to the delivery room.

By the time the doctor had arrived, he had just in time to put on his gloves and shield and to catch our precious little son in his hands. When I heard him cry, it was a sweet sound to me, as I'd not heard Donna cry. Mike's arrival began a new segment of our lives.

Soon after Mike's birth we moved back to Champaign where we made a new life for ourselves. Donna and Mike grew as we struggled to keep our family safe and together. Paul lost his job with the Fuller Brush company. Times were changing and other jobs were hard to find.

The Vietnam war was still going on and the economy was shrinking. Paul found part-time jobs here and there, and finally we had to move to a less-expensive house.

One day Paul called me and asked me to call the man who had sold us our first house—we had to move again. I called the man and asked if there were any houses available. He asked me how we were doing and I broke down and told him our sad story. He immediately saw what our needs were and told me to tell Paul to put on his best suit and to show up for work the next day. They had an opening as a sales person for the housing firm he worked for.

Within a few days we'd moved to one of Weller's cracker-box houses and I thought of Mom and her experience with housing during war time. We lived there for a couple of years amid roaches that when you bug bombed them, would run to another house only to come back when that house was bug bombed.

During that time, Paul found out we qualified for a VA Loan. We were so happy. We could have our own house, again. It took another year, but we finally built a three-bedroom ranch in a good section of town. I still remember, how the kids, finding out we were going to have a carpeted living room, came in and laid down on it and ran their hands back and forth, feeling the soft rug. We have made that house our home for 40-some odd years.

When our children were young, around the age of five and eight, our daughter Donna was told to take her five-year old brother for a wagon ride. Well, she wasn't in the mood for doing such a thing, so she told him that if he would pull her in the wagon to the corner, she'd pull him back. Mike, thinking that would be great, pulled, and tugged and pushed and finally got the wagon with his sister to the corner of our street. She got out and he got in and before he knew what had happened, his big sister left him high and dry, sitting in a wagon he'd had to pull up the street.

He was an angry little boy, and when he finally got back to the house, he came bursting in to tell me all about it. His big sister thought it was funny and giggled—which made him cry. I'm not sure whether I gave her a spanking on the bottom or sent her to her room, but let's just say it didn't happen again.

Time has a way of taking care of things, and when they were out riding bikes one day Donna wasn't watching where she was going. I think she was trying to show off and she hit a rock. Kerplop! She went down and she was on her back under the bike with a skinned ankle and other ouchies! Mike tried to pull the bike off of her, but she said, "Go get Mom!" So he obeyed her, promptly dropping the bike, leaving her under it. I guess you could say it was a payback. He did come get me, of course. We still tease them about the two incidents, and we all get a chuckle out of it.

One of the things that happened in our son's life, that didn't lead to a chuckle, was a serious health problem. Mike was ready to go into 7th grade and a physical was needed to enroll him in school. We took him to his pediatrician. Again, we'd gotten one that was on the ball. After examining

Mike, he told me that he'd found an uneven heartbeat and wanted to do a further test on our son. Just the word "heart problem" sent shivers down my back. The test was run and it was found he had a hole the size of a quarter between his upper chambers and one of the valves was not closing, so the blood was backwashing. We were told he would have to undergo surgery.

Just the thought of him going through surgery scared the pedinkers out of Paul and me. We had a choice of Chicago Children's or Cardinal Glennon Children's Hospital in St. Louis. After much thought and prayer, and a blessing given to him by our Bishop, we chose Cardinal Glennon.

The staff was so kind and helpful. They talked with Mike, telling him and showing him what would happen, and though it was very scary, he was a trouper. There were shots that had to be given to him in his legs and we knew they hurt. His little fingers were pricked so many times to draw blood—to make sure the shots were boasting his immune system—that he had little bandages on all of his fingers. This was to insure he would have enough of his own blood to use, and people from our church, and friends, donated blood in case he needed it.

On the day of the operation we walked the underground tunnel that led from the Children's hospital to the large University Hospital where the operation was to take place. As we sat in the waiting room, there were other parents waiting to hear about their children with similar operations. I remember reading my scriptures, and how one lady asked how could I be so calm. I told her of my faith in God, and that I knew he would protect our little boy. At that moment, I knew she needed someone to be stronger than she was, and that time with her gave me strength as I was helping someone else.

Soon after we had been talking, our doctor came in and said the operation was over and our son was doing well. We were led to a room where Mike laid in a tent of clear plastic. There in a sectioned-off room with curtains, oxygen was being pumped into the tent where there were wires and tubes leading in and out of his little body. His chest was red with the swabs of anti-bacterial liquid. My husband looked at him and turned white as a sheet, and retreated to the hallway. I knew what to expect. I'd just gotten my Nurses Assistance license and had seen things of this sort at the hospital I had worked in. I sat down by our son and held his hand. When he woke up, he said, "Is it all over? Can I have some ice cream?"

I told him he could have ice cream just was soon as the doctor said it was O.K. With that in mind, he drifted off to sleep and we were told we could come back later and visit. When he finally got his own room, I stayed in it with him the first two nights. As the week went by he gained strength and had a heathy appetite, so much so that he said he was tired of hospital food and asked if he could have a hamburger. We were given permission to bring in one for him and he loved it. While he was in the hospital, cards came from everywhere, and one of his best friend's family sent him a package consisting of a card for every day he was to be there. It was great for him to open up those cards each day and enjoy what they had written inside. Sometimes it was a puzzle, or a joke or just something to read. While he was recuperating, a woman would come around and give him something to make. One item was a sock monkey. We still have that silly little monkey!

After two weeks, the doctors couldn't believe the progress Mike had made. Most children stayed for several weeks, but he had healed so fast that after his stitches were taken out we took him home.

I'm sure that wasn't the best ride he'd ever had. We had a car that had seats that dropped down and became flat. It was probably one of the first that came out with that feature. We laid down many quilts and blankets for him to lay on, with a pillow for his head, and we drove the three-hours from St. Louis home. It wasn't the last drive we'd make there and back, but it was the most memorable for him. Just to be going home was a big thing and I think how courageous he was to go through all of that. He told us one time that he would never go into a hospital ever again, not even to visit someone. He'd really disliked the whole thing, but he grew up to eat those word, for when he got married and had his first child, he again entered a hospital and had a sweet experience of seeing the child being born.

After a couple of years passed and he got a clean bill of health, Mike decided to take up cross-country running and weight lifting. He excelled at both of them, and at a competition later on in his life he weight-lifted almost 240 lbs.—double his weight. He went on to cross country, bike riding, and ran in several marathons in Arizona where he now lives. His courage, fortitude, and like his sister, his deep faith in God is what carried him through all of what he has gone through in his life. Now, after a mission for our church, and a B.A. degree from college, he's a talented man in the graphic and advertising field—working for a large auto group in Phoenix, Arizona. He also has made his mark by designing two books for me.

I think we are given challenges in this life for us to overcome, accomplish and to make us grow strong. It's like that old say, "What doesn't kill you will make you stronger," might apply here. All I know is that we can do anything we put our minds to and be triumphant—whether it be a small thing or something more lasting and challenging. I wrote the following poem in honor of all those little ones in our lives that have challenges.

Michael, "Mike" Osborn
and
Donna Osborn.

## The Challenge

He knew it would be hard trying to do it,
His parents told him he couldn't do what he had planned
They said, You might as well consider it canned
But he would not give up the quest
He knew that if he did his best
The task could be completed
And the challenge defeated
He worked and strained and thought
It was tough, but so was he and he fought and fought,
until at last the task was done
The Challenge to be won
As he walked up to get his reward
His tiny steps taking him even more forward
At last it was there in sight
The thing he had worked for within his fight
Yes, such a special prize for such a little one
His very first hotdog on a bun

# A Song and a Pig

Have you ever had one of those days, when you wake up and life seems so exciting? A day when you just want everything to go right? Then as time goes by it sort of dissolves?

Many years ago, in the 1980s, I had the opportunity to audition for a famous country western star by the name of Porter Waggoner. You all probably know him from his connection with Dolly Parton. He was having auditions for his show in Nashville. The auditions were held in different cities and one was our fair little midwest Illinois city. I didn't have a band to back me, but my sister-in-law's husband had a band and they agreed to help me. One of the problems that occurred, though, was that they had practiced the song where they lived and I had practiced the song where I lived—and we hadn't gotten together. That, and the fact that I had totally picked the wrong song for me to sing didn't really help, either. Back then Tanya Tucker's *Delta Dawn* was a top song and I figured it would be great to give it my spin.

Unfortunately, my spin was not in-sync with the beat of the band and we didn't do so well. My dream of going to Nashville was struck down with one fell swoop of, "That was nice. Please wait in the holding area for the final vote."

It's at that point you want to say, "But I can sing another song. Let me try, again. I can do better!" The band was disappointed, even though he said they sounded good. We just didn't have it together and that's why we should have practiced, practiced and practiced more.

Now you might say, "Where does the pig come in?" I'm coming to that. We were ask to stay for a final vote, and we still had hopes that we'd done better than the rest, but when a farmer in overalls came in with his dancing pig act, my heart sank. I could see by the look on Mr. Waggoner's face. He was amused and entertained and we were sunk for sure. Oh yes, why hadn't I just gotten up there and dance a little and sing and roll over, maybe that would have done it. *Somewhere,* I thought, *is a woman that has made it and it's not me. Somewhere a darn pig will be giving the show of his life and it's right here in my own backyard!*

When all the scores were added up and votes came in, we were actually surprised that we came in second, but the winner was—you guessed it, the PIG. There was a brief time, when something came over me, and I just wanted to kick that pig right over the moon.

To say we were ecstatic we came in second would be an understatement, because if the pig had gotten sick we would have been the next choice—providing we would practice more and chose another song.

It must be evident to you by now, that this is about doing things right and of course the only way you can do things right is to practice. You have to practice your music to make it sound beautiful. You have to practice reading to understand the message, and you have to practice everyday of your life to keep it running right on track. Practicing is like breathing. Take a breath in, and exhale, and practice the things you want to accomplish, until it becomes a part of you and with it you can achieve more than you ever dreamed. I didn't become a famous singer, but I finally found my thing to practice.

# Bicycles and Cars, Cars, Cars

As our kids grew up, along came those things all kids want. For Mike it was a bicycle. Not just any bike, but a dirt bike. It was shorter in frame and had special handlebars and no fenders. He took great delight in riding it everywhere. Most of all, it was a great jumping bike and he and some of his friends would go over to the dirt hills just beyond our subdivision and jump those hills. The whole idea was to ride as fast as you could, then as you reach the top of the hill jump the bike up in the air and sail as far as possible—coming down on the back wheel. There were many times when he'd come home with scrapes of all kinds because a jump didn't go well.

As he got older, Mike reached the age where he wanted a car. We told him he would have to work for it. He got a part-time job at the Country Club, and after saving up enough, he and his dad bought a used car. What a car it was—a 1973 Plymouth Roadrunner. Big and somewhat of a muscle car, it ate gas like it was steak. Unfortunately, it was a hard car to handle for a young man of sixteen. He even painted a Roadrunner bird on the upper side panel. A few years later he sold it and bought a 1969 Chevy SS. It was bright yellow with a big black stripe going down though it. It had belonged to a friend of his, and it was a good car. He loved that car and showed it at car shows. It was that car that took us across the country to Utah in what seemed like a never-ending trip, because we'd gone to rescue Donna from a bad situation.

Later on, as he got older, that car was sold and he bought a Chevy S-10. By that time he was in college and working. He decided to paint that truck, and what a job it was. On the hood of the truck was a picture of the engine, so real you thought you could reach right in and touch it. He made it look like a big zipper opening up to reveal an engine. Sad to say he traded that one off before he left for Arizona. For a few years I saw it around town and then it disappeared. It was a sad time for me. That truck was a memory I cherish.

During the 1984 car-buying season, our daughter Donna, three years older than Mike, decided she wanted a car, too. So she and I went out and found a cute little car. Dark Green and smaller, we brought this old Maverick home. I think my husband and son thought we were crazy. It had been modified and someone had dropped a bigger engine in it. It had a lot more power than a young woman should have to have to handle and changing the spark plugs was a nightmare. Either Mike would have to crawl over the side and hang down and change them because he had smaller hands, or Paul would have to drop the motor mounts to get in there. As time went on, Donna, too, changed cars and we all enjoyed a more settled time with our vehicles.

I think my favorite car of that era was our 1987 Pontiac Grand Prix. It was the last of the great cars that had long lines and style. We bought it used, so it was a couple of years old. It was silver and it drove like a dream. The engine was clean and we kept it that way. One day while Mike was working on his truck, he got the idea to paint the Pontiac another color, so he took the bottom half and painted it a deep wine red. Oh, was it beautiful and we took it to a couple of car shows when he took his S-10, to show off. It was fun and we got many wows, ohs and ahs with it. We even took it across the country on a trip, but the time had come for us to say goodbye to a time and era that had long since gone as did the classic cars of our lives. We enjoyed driving a beautiful Cadillac CTS—and our present car, a Lincoln MKS. I still prefer the Cadillac. It is a true breed of it's own.

In our lives we all have those things we like to have, whether it be a car, a favorite chair or a vase, but there comes a time when all they are just possessions. We can enjoy them for a while and then they must be passed on or sold for someone else to enjoy. What we can keep are friendships.

We can't keep them like things to be put on display. Instead, they are something we can cherish, nurture and enjoy forever.

Above: Mike's 1969 Chevy SS.
Below: Our 1987 Grand Prix.

# Nurses, Subs and Candy

During the middle 1980s, I took courses to become a Nurse's Assistant. It was a means to an end, and I had always wanted be in the medical field. I knew I was really too old to go back to a full-time nursing school, but I felt this would do. I graduated from what was then Mercy Hospital and had my license in hand. At first, I worked up on the pediatric floor, but then I was moved to the geriatric floor. I loved being around the children, and the new-born babies. However, I seemed to have a good rapport with the older set. So when I finally went away from Mercy I started working at a nursing home. It was a general one, and the hours were awful. I worked the swing shift, which meant I would go in at 11:00 p.m. one day, have a break, and then do the 3:00 p.m., and 11:00 p.m. the day afterward. I had a hard time sleeping in the daytime, even though everyone was gone to school or working. I'm not sure what happened, but a patient with a bacterial infection had been cleared by the doctor to not wear a mask anymore. Well, I came down with something that I thought was a very bad cold. I couldn't get better and had to call in sick. By the time I saw a doctor of my own, I was running a high temperature and he put me in the hospital in isolation. I had one lung that was ready to collapse and it hurt to breathe. It took several days in the hospital before I began to feel human again. Then I was told that I could not work in a medical facility for at least a year.

That was enough to topple my world. I took the time to recuperate, and a year later I got a job in a drugstore—in the cosmetic section as I had listed Hairdresser and Cosmetologist. I worked there for a couple of years, but after being robbed, I decided it was just not for me. And I was still struggling with my health.

Finally, our friend Betsy told us they were opening a Soup'n'Sub place out at the local mall. Knowing I loved to cook, Betsy figured that it would be right down my ally. I loved working there. I was given some freedom and I created two sandwiches that I still make today for my family.

Our daughter Donna and our son Michael worked there, too. Everyday was a joy at work, baking the bread, making up soups. And the hours were good. I worked part-time in the morning to 2:00 p.m. After almost two years of working there, Donna and I were told the shop might be closing as the rent had gone up and they could no longer keep it afloat. They sold it to someone else. Donna and I were disappointed. When the new owner took over, it just wasn't the same place. He was not a very good boss and lacked the skills to run a place like that.

I was working my last few weeks there, when I saw a new little shop opening up next door. I inquired if they were hiring and they said they were. Within a few days I gave my notice that I was moving on, and started working at the new place.

The new store was a craft shop, and since Mom and I were into making crafts, it seemed like a great job to have. Again, I'd found a place where I loved working. Pat was a wonderful woman, and was a good boss and fair to us all. I got to sell some of Mom's crafts, making her a little money, too.

One day I found out the next day was Pat's Birthday. I had a habit of writing poems for people for different occasions, so I wrote one for her. I framed it and gave it to her. She loved it and asked if I had any more. I said yes and soon I was selling poems, in decorated frames. This went on for quite sometime.

During this time, there was a candy store across the isle from us. It wasn't just any candy store. it was Fannie May. We'd go over and get free samples, and sometimes I'd pick up a piece or two to nibble on when times at the store got slow.

One day I noticed some young fellows messing around at the counter.

The woman who worked there was older and had her back turned to them filling up candy boxes. I tried to get her attention by calling her, thinking she would answer the phone—but she didn't. About that time I saw one of them take one of the sample boxes off a display stand and off they went. I called Mall Security and when they came down I pointed out where the boys had gone. They caught them out in the parking lot trying to eat the candies. What they didn't know was that those candies were old and had gone to sugar. They looked good on the outside, but were bad on the inside. They got hauled away for minor theft and I got a free box of candy for my efforts.

Soon after that, was a day that topped the "theft" one. The mall always had promotions going on and close to the Sears store, where we were, they had a celebrity come and sign his book. He was the fellow who still plays Thorn Forester on the *Bold and Beautiful* television show. There must have been half the women of the city show up for the event.

They were lined all the way back to the middle of the mall. One of the little-old ladies who worked at the candy shop just had a hissy fit over the fact that he was going to be there and though she was so close, but couldn't leave her store. She hailed down one of the security men and told him to give the man who played Thorn the chocolate-covered roses she'd set aside.

She watched, as did I, as the young, middle-aged and older women had their pictures taken with him, or had the book signed, while we just sat there and waved at each other—shrugging our shoulders and thinking to ourselves, *What fun that must be.*

When everything was almost over and the crowd had gone, the actor made his way over to the candy store and landed a big kiss on the old lady's cheek. I thought she was going to faint right there in his arms. I, on the other hand, only got a quick wave and a "Hi" from him.

*Well*, I thought to myself, *that's O.K.* I have my handsome husband to go home to and she was a lonely woman who, for a moment, had something extraordinary happen to her that would become one of her cherished memories. As for me I was just happy to have seen a famous person and enjoy a candy or two in the process.

We did have good days sales that day and I have to say it was very worthwhile, sitting there as a watcher and not a doer for once. I think my favorite place to work though had to be the sub shop.

## For Your Pleasure—The Tuna Deluxe

2 cans of albacore tuna, well drained

2 tbsp. Pickle relish

1 tsp. of a brand named herb season mix

2 tbsp. minced green onion

1/2 cup of shredded cheddar cheese

1/3 cup real mayonnaise

Butter softened

Your choice of bread. I prefer whole wheat or rye.

Mix all ingredients together *except* the butter in a medium bowl and set in the refrigerator for 1 hour. Then spread the tuna on the bread, topping it with another piece of bread. Butter well and brown on both sides in a large skillet set on med-high setting. When all is browned well and the cheese is melting, remove, cut in half and serve with a pickle or I liked to stick on top, a couple of black olives on a toothpick for decoration.

# A New Member of the Family & A New Friend

About a year after we all worked at the sub shop, our son moved away. Believe you me, when I say that was one of the hardest things I've ever had experienced. He was on his way to a new state, a new home and eventually a young woman in his life. We were working on our first book, and having trouble getting it all together—with him in Arizona and me in Illinois. He decided to fly back to Illinois, but time was short and he only had a weekend. He told us he was bringing someone else along with him and we figured it was the young woman. We were right. We met in Chicago, as it was easier for them, and it meant we would not lose precious time as we could work on the book.

At first I was apprehensive of her. After all, he was my only son and well, mothers tend to be a little possessive of their only sons, as I was of Donna—our only girl.

Kimberly was a lovely young thing, bright and poised. I thought to my-self, *Val, this is it. She's the one.* I could see by the way their eyes lit up when they looked at each other that she would soon be the woman in his life and I would have to stand back and let that happened. I can't say it was easy, as I struggled to let go and let her take over, but in the years that have gone by, I've gotten to know and love her as if she were my own child. To-gether they have made a sweet, safe home for our five grandchildren, and she welcomes us into their home with open arms.

Cutting the apron strings is the hardest thing a mother can do, and yet there's so much to be gained by it. A whole new world opens up to you, and you feel a part of a bigger picture. It's all how we perceive things and people. It's also a good reason to never judge a box by its outside—inside, you might find a rare gem.

Speaking of rare gems reminds me that while we were in Chicago, we'd stayed overnight, visiting and doing some sightseeing. We went to the Museum of Art and stopped by the Chicago LDS Temple. The next day we went to church. After getting settled into a pew we noticed a man and his family making their way down to a pew a few rows ahead of us. The man looked familiar and I nudged Paul and Mike. "Isn't that Donny Osmond?" Paul said he didn't think so, but when the man turned around to speak to someone behind him, sure enough it was. Well, I can tell you, I had a hard time keeping my mind on the service. My daughter had followed his career and sent him letters in her early tween and teen years. His family had kindly sent us letters back, and how special that was to us as a family. After worship service was over and we were on our way to Sunday School, I kept thinking, *What if we run into him, what would I say?* After all, he was an international star, and I remembered his starring in *Joseph and the Amazing Technicolor Coat* while in Chicago. And just as we turned the corner—I nearly ran into him.

There he was—ushering people into the Sunday School Class. I gathered up my courage and said, "Brother Osmond, I want to tell you how much we have loved your music and what a wonderful influence you've had on our family." Then I told him briefly about the letters. He was so gracious and kind. He even gave us all a hug and a handshake. Not thinking, I'd not taken my camera with me to get that special picture.

As we settled in to the little room that was our class, I thought, *WOW! I just got a hug from Donny Osmond, and my daughter, one of his biggest fans, has missed this special time.* As we waited, our teacher came in—and it was Donny! *Well this is just icing on the cupcake*, I thought, *Could things not get any better, today?*

He looked around the room, welcoming all the visitors to class, and then said, "Now we need someone to say the opening prayer." As he said that, the hair raised on the back of my neck. I could feel his eyes heading my way. Then he said in that smooth voice of his, "Sister Osborn, will you do the honors?" I nodded, yes, and then said the nicest prayer and sat down. My heart was beating so fast I thought everyone could have heard it in that little room.

His lesson was wonderful and as we parted ways he said, "You know the names Osmond and Osborn are similar. I'll bet your family came from England. We might just be related!" I agreed with him and thought, *if only that were true.*

It had been an extraordinary weekend. Not only had I met Donny Osmond, but I was about to gain a new daughter and how precious was all of this. Yes, gems do come in all sizes and shapes and the most precious of all was indeed the gem of a growing family.

Michael and Kimberly Osborn at their
Wedding Reception, Farmington, New Mexico, February 3, 1995.

Kimberly and Michael Osborn on their Wedding Day
Mesa, Arizona, February 3, 1995.

# Grandkids, Bubbles, Lipstick and Giggles

Grandchildren can be so much fun—from their first smile, the first step and the first word. I'm fortunate to have some wonderful grandchildren and so I write these short stories about them so that one day, when they read this, they will have memories, too, and pass them on to their children.

Most of us who have grandchildren know what a joy they can be. They're so much fun and do such crazy things at times. The best part is that if things go wrong, you know the dirty diaper, the upchuck, or tantrum, you can just hand them back to the parents.

When they're little it's fun to dress them up and coo over them, but at they grow up we began to see their different personalities coming of each as more work was put into the precious time we got to spend with them. Having grandchildren hundreds of miles away from you makes it much harder to establish those ties that bind us to them. But over the years we've been able to make those trips, building wonderful memories of out time with them.

When our only granddaughter Shayla was just about three months old the family, on both sides, went out to visit. She was to have her baby blessing. We were all sitting around and she was laying on the floor. One of her aunts, on her mother's side, decided to dress her up in a little tu tu and a cute little bathing suit—all pretty and pink. She then placed a big pair of sunglasses her little face and the sight was enough to make us all giggle. Now she's older and we respect our young granddaughter for her beauty and her intellect.

When Shayla went into 6th grade, Paul and I went out to Arizona to visit. She was in a Science Fair at school, and working on a project to find stains and then find the cleanser, or home remedies, would take the stains out. She was having a problem with removing blood from white material. She asked me what would I use. I told her that hydrogen peroxide would surely take it out. She kind laughed and thought this old Grandma had lost her marbles, but promised she would try it. The next day, when we went to see her display, she told me I was right. She couldn't believe how fast it cleaned it up.

Her project was wonderful and she received a second-place ribbon. How proud we were of her. She is growing up so fast in front of our eyes—into a confident young lady.

She is her parents' and our princess. Besides her mother she is the only girl in a family of all boys and if you don't think that's a challenge —you have another think coming!

Baby Shayla Renee Osborn
1996,

# Bubble, Bubble, Double Trouble

In the summer of 2009, our son, his wife and their family of five kids came back to visit and to celebrate my parents 70th Anniversary.

We have a big backyard for the kids to play in and they had fun with balls, sidewalk chalk and bubbles we'd given them to play with outside. It was all going great until my daughter-in-law and I looked out the window and saw an enormous amount of fluffy bubbles pouring out of my waterfall and pond. We asked all the children who was to blame. We told them we weren't angry. They all denied it, but little Jeffery stood back, looking very guilty. Since he was one with a habit of getting into trouble, we decided it was probably him. We said he would have to help clean it up and that there would be no dessert for him that night. He was one very sad little boy.

Suppertime came and we all sat down to eat. The meal was enjoyed by all—except one of the children. Our oldest grandson Glenn wasn't eating his usual portion and we wondered if he was sick. I went to get the dessert and asked if he would like to help. While in the kitchen he said, "Grandma, I don't think I want any desert."

"Why is that?" I asked.

"I don't deserve it. I'm the one who put the bubbles in the pond."

"Oh Glenn, what ever possessed you to do that?" I asked.

"I don't know. It seemed like a fun thing to do at the time, but when I saw how many bubbles came out, and it started to overflow, I kind of got scared."

"It's all right, It's not anything that can't be fixed with fresh water. It's just a good thing there weren't real fish in there. Now help me put dessert on the table and we'll talk about this after supper to see what came be done."

After supper we talked, and Glenn decided he would clean out the pond and help in the garden to make up for his fun mistake. He's growing up to be a responsible young man now, with a love for soccer, baseball, and camping out. He's also learning to play a mean clarinet.

The pond has since been replaced with a lovely statue with flowers around it, but I still can look at the corner of the backyard and get a good chuckle remembering those bubbles.

Our backyard, after the pond was removed,
but the memory of Glenn's honesty still brings a smile.

# Shut the Box

It isn't always easy teaching children new games and how to play fair. All they know is that they want to win—all the time! Our special middle grandchild Austin loves playing games. He will play Dot-dot. Hangman, loves soccer and just about anything you put in front of him, and he seems to pick up the rules very well.

A few years back, when he was about seven, we got a game called *Shut The Box*. It's a simple, interactive board game. You just roll two dice in a wooden box that has wooden keys set along the top numbered 1 through 12. The idea is to roll and then flip up the number you've rolled or any combination. I wasn't sure Austin was ready for this game, but his mother assured me he was good at math.

I showed him how to play and off we went at it. Well, from the first round he did really well, and by the time the game was almost over, he was far ahead of me in the least points accumulated. I thought to myself, *This kid is really good at this*.

By the time we were down to the next to last round, I knew I was in trouble and would surely lose the game. I gave my next-to-last roll of the dice and almost prayed that it would roll the twelve I needed to win. What can I say? No sooner had the dice left my hand when I thought, *I've got it in the bag. There's no way he can win now*. I only had one more roll, and if I could get a six, I'd beat him. The dice tumbled and tumbled and came to rest. There they sat—looking up at me with a ten. I couldn't do any more. It was his turn.

Austin gave those dice roll after roll, and flipped up number after number, until he came down to his last roll. He had a big 12 that he would have to roll. He tumbled those dice out of his little hands and they came to rest in the middle of the box. I about fell off my chair. There was a big 12. He had snookered me out of the game and won, won, won, as he put it. He danced around the room shouting, "I won! I won!" I gave him his prize, a piece of candy. He gave me a great big hug and off he ran to tell his mom.

Life has all kinds of games we can play, some bring us joy, and some are best left alone or they might get us in trouble. Life also has a way of giving us the best rewards. Some of the best I've received are the smiles and hugs our Austin gives to me.

Austin, Glenn and Jeffrey Osborn
"A yummy treat."

# The Whirlwind

Of the four grandsons there is Jeffery. Jeffery has a way of just looking at trouble and it comes running. In his young years of three and four, he single-handedly got into more trouble than his other brothers. His innate curiosity always seem to rear it ugly head and well, you would find him in places where he shouldn't be.

While visiting us one time—he disappeared. When we found him, he'd gotten into my vanity and sitting on the bed he'd painted himself black with my mascara brush, managing to pour out almost a full bottle of my best perfume, not only on himself, but all over the floor. To this day I can still walk in that room and smell Ming Shu perfume. Later, he became skilled at painting with his mother's lipstick all over the TV the floor of their family room, and himself.

One day I came into the kitchen of their home and found him stuffing himself with Mommy's best candies. I told him, "No, Jeffery." He promptly whacked me in the tummy. If you come from my generation, you might say a good spank on the bottom would stop him, but not Jeffery. He had a way of becoming more defiant.

It took lots patience for all of us, and as time went on we thought it would all blow over. Then one day, Jeffery got mad at me for telling him to be careful and not throw things over the kitchen counter where he was sitting. He proceeded to throw a fork that nearly hit me. That's when Grandma 101 kicked in and I picked him up and took him back to his room, put him on his bed and gave him a good talking to. At first he fought it, but when I finally said, "Okay, if that's the way you want it, then Grandma will walk out that door and never come back to see you."

I got up and walked toward the hall. He was still whining, so I simply went out the door, shutting it behind me, but it made me cry, so I went to the bathroom to dry my eyes. It broke my heart that I had to talk to him that way, but I wanted to get across to him that if you do something bad there are consequences. I heard him shout, "No," and he kicked the wall, as I walked down the hallway.

I went out to tell our daughter-in-law what had happened and she went back to talk with him. When he came back out of his room, he was quiet, meek, and he apologized to me. Later in the evening, when we were getting ready to leave and go back to the place we were staying, we gave all the kids a hug. When it came his turn, he gave me the tightest bear hug and said, "Grandma, please don't leave me, I love you." I assured him we would be back the next day, and he gave me another hug. Since that day, when we come to visit Jeffery is the one to give us the biggest hugs.

Sometimes, grandparents have the job of being "the bad guy" and of disciplining our grandchildren. It wasn't too long after Jeffery's problems that Glenn and Austin were being really noisy and rowdy. I walked into their room and said, "Quiet down, all of you. Grandma's not feeling well, and you don't want to make Grandma mad. You never know what I might do." Well, I guess it sunk in because later, when his two younger brothers were going at it again, Glenn said, "You'd better cut that out. You never know what Grandma might do!" Hallelujah! They'd seen the light!

Whirwind Jeffery Osborn,
about three years old.

# Giggles and Tickles

Our youngest Grandson is the sweetest thing. He also loves being right in the middle of things. If there's anything worthy of his attention—he's right there. He loves to play games, and even if he doesn't know how to play, he will try.

Not to long ago we were visiting our son, daughter-in-law and grandkids. When we arrived there was a flurry of hugs and, "So glad you're here."

Our littlest grandson, Adam, came dashing out to greet us with a big hug and an attempt to tickle us. Well, neither of us are ticklish, and so it didn't work. I think he was a bit disappointed, but just a little while later he came out with a big smile on his face to the dinning room where I was sitting. He climbed up on my lap and continued to try to tickle me again. I could see he wasn't going to stop at it, so I tickled him instead, and he flashed the biggest smile and lots of giggles. All that day he would come up to his grandfather and me and it would become a ticklefest all over.

I've never seen a child who smiles bigger then Adam. Joy just flows from him. So do tears—when an older brother takes away his toys, or tries to overrun him on a game. However Adam seems to have a simple way of finding joy in everything he does. All through our two-week stay, every day he would attempt to tickle us and then run like crazy giggling all the way. His laughter was contagious and we all found ourselves laughing at his little antics.

Sometimes the simplest things mean the most. The laughter of a child, little games played with them, bubbles in the pond, and a child that is bright and smart. There's a saying we all know, "Laughter is the best medicine." In all cases with our grandkids, we've had lots of love and much laughter. We wouldn't change it for all the money in the world.

Above: Glen, Jeff and Austin Osborn.

Adam Osborn, the boy in
the mirror.

Shayla Osborn playing her
flute at Great-grandparents
Huffman's 70th wedding
anniversary.

Our Osborn grandchildren:
Austin, Adam, Shayla, Glen and Jeff.

# Friends of all Kinds Flock Together

I've had many acquaintances in my life, and only a few truly good friends—the kind that come over and see you through an illness, take you to a Dolly Parton concert or sit in a old theater watching a goofy movies, like *Masters of the Universe,* and be the one throwing popcorn at the kids. These are stories about some of those wonderful people that are no longer with me—and those that still are.

A few years ago we started to meet together. Most of us were over 60 and it became like a club. We didn't have a name for our group until one of the women said, "We aren't cougars anymore, but we've got lot of wisdom among all of us."

I asked, "You mean we're wiley like foxes?"

That's it! Most of us have silver hair, so why not call our group the Silver Foxes. Well, the name has stuck and we all enjoy a lunch out every month, where we can talk about our families, show pictures, exchange a recipe or two, and just laugh and be ourselves—The wise and wiley Silver Foxes.

# Talent, Talent, Talent

There are people who walk into your life path and remain there for a while, and there are those who go away all too soon but leave a lasting memory. In my life, I've had both. They've made impressions, not only upon my mind, but in my heart. Mary was one of those people. She was outgoing, cooked wonderfully, sewed, canned, made wedding cakes, quilted and grew her own garden. She raised three beautiful girls, had chickens, goats, and even buffalo at one time or another. She knew all about plants: how to use them, their medicinal properties, and she taught me how to make jelly from the flowers of the violet plant. Amazing!

We did fun things together, went to movies, laughed at stupid stuff and on one occasion, we went on a trip to a *Star Trek* convention in Indianapolis. It was fun to see all the people dressed in *Star Trek* garb. We only wore our badges. We bought some stuff, and then we went to listen to and meet Patrick Stewart the actor who played Captain Picard on *Star Trek Generations*.

That was a thrill and we often recalled it. When Mary left us, it was way too soon. Diabetes took her. Even thought she was diligent with her medications, shots and testing, it still prevailed. She struggled and fought the good fight. She set an example for me that I may never be able to achieve, but the challenge she gave me still rings in my mind and heart—endure to the end. I miss her and still reach for the phone thinking I can talk with Mary and everything will be OK. I dedicate the following poem to her memory.

## One Day At A Time

Whatever the goals you're pursuing
No matter how rugged the climb
You're certain to get there
by trying your best,
and taking it one day at a time.
Forever is hard to imagine
The future may seem far away,
But every new dawn
brings a wonderful chance
to do what you can
to make you advance
One day at a time.

A sample of friend
Mary's wonderful
wedding cakes.

## Poems and Pantyhose

Then there was Pat Lamb, my dear friend, my mentor and a sweet woman. She taught me the basics of writing prose and poems. She even wrote a book of her own called *Diamonds by the side of the Road*. Pat encouraged me to take classes at the local Junior college to improve my writing skills. It was she who helped me with my first book. We slaved over two computers to get the story right and finally found a company who would publish it. When the book was finished, and we had it in our hands, we rejoiced over a feat accomplished. I often pick up her book of poems and read those sweet thought of hers. My favorite memory, though, has to be her pantyhose story.

She had put on dress and a pair of pantyhose one day as she had a meeting to go to. She thought the pantyhose seemed a bit loose, but she was in a hurry and so she pulled them up a little higher and thought her elastic-waisted slip would help hold them up. She made it though the meeting, and on her way home she stopped by the store to get some food for supper. As she walked down one of the isles she found herself feeling a bit strange, like she was walking *on* something. She looked down and there, hanging around her feet, were those silly pantyhose. "Oh my," she said to herself. She thought about reaching down and pulling them back up, but she knew that wouldn't work, so right there in the isle of the store, she gracefully took off her shoes, looked around, and removed those pantyhose—quickly stuffing them into her purse. I still have visions of her sitting there telling this story with tears of laughter running down our faces.

I'll miss her smile and her quiet way of getting the message across—whatever it would be—and those wonderful stories of hers. She has gone on to a great reward that had been set aside for her.

# Pheasant, Dinner and Thee

There are other people, that are making such sweet new memories. One of those, is a woman in our lives who has became like another mother for my husband Paul. His mother and father died in the 1970s and '80s and though he had my mom and dad to fall back on, he missed them terribly. His mother's name was Elizabeth, but everyone called her Betty.

In the early 1990s, we met another Betty—Betty N., and her husband Lyle. Lyle took to my husband right away and often called him "son." When Lyle died, he told his wife Betty N. that he had another son called Paul. She wasn't sure what he meant but then it hit her—it was my Paul. She took him under her wing and always looked upon him as her son, too, especially after she found out he'd lost his mother, Betty O.

Betty N., an outspoken woman, said what she thought. One day when we were visiting her she told us a story. It was about a time when food was short and sometimes you had to eat what the good Lord presented to you. It was on such an occasion, as she was driving home from work one day, that she hit a pheasant with her car and stunned it. She stopped the car, got out and looked at the pheasant. It was flailing around and she simple made the choice of breaking its neck, taking it home, dressing it and cooking it for supper.

When Lyle came home she presented her meal to him. He said, "What in the world is that?"

She said, "It's pheasant for thee and me for supper." Well, they feasted that night, and it was good. Betty has kept us amused, loved and advised. She will always be our Betty—a second mother to Paul. She has a special place in our hearts. I love the saying: "Mother are angels in disguise." It certainly applies with Betty N.

# Lasting Friendships

Other friends are also like family, so much we wish they really were part of our family. Bonnie is one of those. I first met her in my Junior year of high school. We became fast friends and often double-dated with our boy friends. Shortly after we'd established a good friendship, she found herself living in an abusive home situation. Her grandmother was fearful for her and asked us if we would take her in as a foster child. Mom and Dad agreed it would be best, and for the first time I had a sister! I was elated! We became two peas in a pod. We went everywhere together, talked late at night, and probably gave Mom more gray hairs early on then she wanted. Mom said it was like having twins in the house. And what a handful we were.

By the time we'd graduated, Bonnie's boyfriend became her fiance and soon after that they were married in the little church my Dad preached in. At first it was a good marriage, but down the line she became more of a servant to him and his mother, and after many years, and when the children were grown, she found her husband had been unfaithful to her and that ended the marriage. Heartbroken, she picked up the pieces of her life and continued on until she met a wonderful man who now treats her like the queen she is and with the respect she deserved.

We still keep in touch by phone and email, and we've had a chance to see each other over the years. I'm so glad I had the experience, if only for short time, of not being an only child. There is a little saying that applies here: "Family and Friends are Forever." For me, I will forever have a sister.

# Here in America

I have a dear friend that came here from Finland. She is outspoken, determined and sometimes a gutsy lady. She also has some very great talents. One of those is searching out and finding great bargains. I've never seen anyone who could walk into Goodwill, or Salvation Army and come out with the best bargains you ever saw.

She would find things that were useful, or that could be resold. She would find material, and yarn, and create beautiful quilts and afghans. She knitted beautiful booties and gloves, scarves and sweaters.

Every year Tepa would get things together for her annual garage sale. Now I don't have to tell you all about how much work goes into putting together a sale. There's all the sorting, marking, tabulating—and then the customers. Oh my! They come from all kinds of cultures and are all sizes and shapes. And all of them are looking for that elusive, but possibly great bargain, or special treasure, maybe even an antique or two.

Tepa's autumn garage sale started around 7:00 a.m. on the eventful day. I had a few things I wanted to get rid of, too. I had brought them over the night before with my table to show the items. The people came in droves. I'd never seen so many in the morning and item after item was sold. Five, two, and some fifty-cents items went fast.

Around 11:00 am on the last day of the sale we marked down several items, but Tepa left two items at the same price: a very lovely set of curtains and some very attractive material. Shortly after the markdown, two returning customers came to look around. Tepa leaned over and said to me, "Now you just wait and watch. They will try to chew me down on the prices after we've already marked them down. They were here last year and I've had dealings with them before."

So I waited and watched, and sure enough, they up to Tepa with the curtains and material.

The older of the two women spoke in broken English, "Five dollar for everything?"

"No," Tepa said firmly. She shifted slightly in her chair to show her authority.

"You sure?" the woman asked. "Five dollar?"

This time I could see Tepa had her fill of these persistent people. She stood up her full height, towering above them, and said in her firm, strong voice with a Finnish accent, "This is America. We do it the American way. No barter. The price is as it says. Take it or leave it!" Then she politely sat down, picked up her bottle of water and took a drink.

I do think those women were in shock! I was in shock! *Wow,* I thought to myself. *She really means business.*

Well, the ladies looked at each other, took the curtains and material back to the table, and looked around a little more.

"Tepa," I said, "how did you know, I mean they really wanted to barter with you."

She replied, "It has always been that way when they come here. I'm used to it. Today, though, I finally said what I was thinking. You watch. They will be back."

Fairly soon, the women came, again, with the curtains and material—and an additional item.

"Five dollar?" they asked again.

Tepa shook her head. "I told you priced as is."

The two women looked at each other, then the older one pulled some money out of her little purse and handed over the ten dollars as Tepa had priced the material and curtains, and the other woman paid for the smaller item she had in her hand. Off they went with their treasures.

Well, I have to tell you, I impressed with how Tepa had handled the situation, but more than that, it was her saying, "We live in America, We do things the American way."

Now how much prouder could I be to have had a friend who came here from another country and took America as her country so seriously that she honored this great nation—even at a garage sale. God Bless dearly departed Tepa. God Bless America!

# Soup, Onions and a Car

A dear friend of mine, Kay, has a son-in-law, DJ, who loves to joke around, and he often pulls a few jokes on her. She's good natured and takes them in stride—and sometimes she has a chance for a little payback.

Now there's one thing DJ hates more than anything else —onions. One day while Kay was at her daughter's home, she decided to make some vegetable soup. DJ loves vegetable soup, but he wants it made without onions. Well, that kind of soup lacks a little without the onions, so she told him she would make it without the onion, however, she said nothing about shallots, garlic or chives. She also was in the middle of packing up lunches for her grandson and for DJ. So she said to herself, "Self let's just see how much he would like an onion in his lunch." So she pulled out a big onion from the refrigerator and carefully wrapped it up in foil. Then she called, "Oh, DJ, your lunch is ready."

He came in and grabbed up his lunch, thanked her and said, "I hope you packed something good."

"Oh my, yes I did," Kay answered innocently. DJ gave her a quick pat on the shoulder and off he went.

Kay went back to the soup and did a few other things around the house for her daughter, waiting for that eventual phone call she knew would come. Indeed it did. Right around noon, the phone rang and she answered it.

At the other end of the phone was DJ with the onion in his hand. "Kay, why?"

"Why, What?" Kay replied. "You know what, this onion in my lunch. I don't like onions!"

"Oh, poor baby. Whatever do you mean?" Kay said, with a grin on her face.

"I thought you'd given me an apple and what do I see? An onion!" DJ said—a higher pitched voice.

"Why DJ, I just couldn't resist giving you something that's really good for you. I thought you'd make a sandwich of it.

By now Kay was at the point of laughing outloud.

"Uh-huh. Well, I'll find a good home for this onion," Suddenly, he could hear her laughing hysterically.

"Oh, I'm really sorry, DJ. I just couldn't resist the chance to pull a joke on you. I hope you're not angry with me."

"Oh Kay, I could never get mad at you. Why you're my sweet mother-in-law," he said. "I'll see you when I get home."

"Okay, deary," Kay replied.

As she hung up the phone Kay got a smile on her face. *Oh yes just wait till you get home*, she thought. *Have I got a surprise for you. I know this may be going a bit to far, but I know he's going to pull a joke on me when he gets home and I just have to do this one more thing.*

Outside in the driveway sat DJ's pride and joy, a collectable 1968 Chevy. She quickly went outside and on the top of the medallion of the hood she place, you guessed it—an onion! That evening, when dear DJ came home, it didn't catch his eye right away, but awhile later Kay said to him, "Oh, DJ, would you see if there's any mail?"

She watched as he lumbered out to the mailbox, still not seeing the onion, but he could smell it. You see, this was in Arizona and it had been a warm day. He had a habit of checking his beloved car and as he did, the smell of the onion just got stronger until—sure enough—he found it.

Now I can't say what happened after that. I think there were some, "What in the world?" and "Who did this?"

However, after the dust had settled, this mild-mannered man simply came back in the house, sat down in his favorite chair, turned on the TV and said nothing. Somewhere out in the kitchen, he could hear someone chuckling and soon the laughter got louder, the tears started to roll down from both his wife's and his mother-in-law's eyes—not from the onion, but from the sheer joy of a practical joke well executed.

I guess somewhere in this story there is a meaning. Perhaps it's "Have an onion a day, it'll keep the doctor and everyone else away," or "A laugh a day will keep that blues away." I want to think it's the latter. So go out there today and do something that will make you chuckle—oh heck—even make you have a good laugh or two. The rewards are wonderful!

My dear and witty friend Kay.

# Faith Beyond Measure

There are people who influence, and sometimes change, the course of your life for a time. Shauna and J.R. were two of these people. They were, and still are, members of our church. When we first met them, I found two dynamic people with one married child and two teen-aged children and J.R. in a wheel chair. I found out that he'd been in a car accident which left him a paraplegic. It was early on in their lives when it happened. Yet there they were—a wonderful example of true love and faith.

One of my favorite memories is the day J.R. and Shauna were to have an outdoor party at their lovely home. The morning started out O.K., and plans were in the process for the evening cookout. In the afternoon, dark clouds started to gather and it looked like there would be no party. But J.R. simply said, "I have prayed to the Lord and it will not rain."

I thought, *That is really a bold statement to make.* But J.R. continued to have the strong faith and impression that it would not rain. People started to gather and the cookout began. The clouds parted and for those three hours there was no rain. We all enjoyed a lovely evening. It wasn't until the last person left, and we were helping clean up, that we saw the clouds gathering again and the first raindrops started to fall.

By the time we'd cleaned up, it was raining fairly hard and by the time we got home it was raining cats and dogs.

The next day I called Shauna to thank her for a wonderful evening. I made a comment about how those clouds just seemed to hang back the whole time. She replied, "Never underestimate the faith of a righteous man and the hand of the Lord in all matters including a little thunderstorm."

After that, I never questioned the love and faith they both showed in all things, even after J.R. was diagnosed with cancer, he continued in faith as

Shauna has since his death.

Faith is something felt, but not always seen by the human eye, and yet it is something we can all have and feel, no matter what or who we believe in, and, like friends, we can keep it in our hearts forever.

J.R. Larsen, professor of Entomology at the University of Illinois and Director of Life Sciences—1983.

# Friends are Forever

During my lifetime, I've met many people, but none as unique as dedicated Sherron. We first met at a church meeting. They were new in town. Her husband Joe, was retired military and a good and jolly guy.

Sherron's life was her children. They had four girls and one boy. It didn't take long before I was at her house almost as much as I was at my own home. We talked for hours, went to movies, sat on their front porch in our coats, handing out Halloween candy. We laughed over "spilt milk," and cried over lost family members. I've seem her go through some really rough times: an operation that came back to haunt her, a spouse with cancer, and her own diagnosis of ovarian cancer. She's battled it for years, and the courage and faith I see in God is amazing. I don't know how this story will pan out, but at the writing of this book, her battle continues. I cherish her friendship and admire the love she's shown to family and friends. There is a saying:

Friendship is a priceless gift
That can't be bought or sold—
But to have an understanding friend
Is worth far more than gold

Sherron is, and will always be, that priceless gift.

# Holidays and Special Occasions

Some of the most joyful times are the holidays. My favorite of all is Christmas. I love Easter, and Valentines Day is nice, but Christmas brings a special feeling, an unexplainable joy and warm feeling that comes over me. Oh the smells of Christmas are wonderful. The carols and Christmas songs brings back such sweet memories.

From the time I was a little girl, I was fascinated with Christmas, not just because of the presents I got, but because it was a time for the family to get together. We would meet at one of the grandparent's homes. Everyone brought a special dish. There would be a ham and turkey. Sometimes rabbit would be served. Mashed potatoes were piled high in big dish near the home-canned green beans. Grandma Kirkpatrick always made her English Plum pudding—a recipe handed down through generations of her family—the Edwards. And there were the pies. Mom bought two—usually an apple, and a pecan. Later, as the family changed she would bring her wonderful Blueberry-Rhubarb pie that our son craved. On top of all of that, there was always homemade noodles, cranberry salad, homemade pickled beets, pickles, Jams—and of course home-baked bread or rolls and candies and cookies.

At Grandma and Grandpa Huffman's, a family gathering, again meant wonderful food, with everyone bringing their special dish. I have to say that Grandma Huffman made the most delicious Fried chicken.

When both of our grandparents passed away, things changed. We started rotating Christmas dinners—on a Sunday other than Christmas Day at Mom's house, and Aunt Dora or Aunt Lucille would take over for alternate Christmas meals. Of course this didn't happen until after Mom and Dad moved back near the homestead in Bismarck.

In our early years of marriage, we would go to Mom and Dad's where ever they were. As a pastor in a church circuit he would be moved occasionally. I remember a special time when we had gone down to Wood River. We just had Donna at the time and she was around two years old. They had a little Boston terrier named Princess who Donna loved to play with. One day we found them both up in the window seat, looking through the window at the outside and watching the people go by. We asked Donna what she was looking for and she replied, "I'm waiting to see Santa." We explained to her that Santa would only come to the house when she was in bed. That evening she insisted on waiting up for Santa. So we put her on the couch and I sat up with her until she fell asleep. Santa came that night, of course, and when she woke up the next morning, there were presents waiting to be unwrapped and the cookies and milk that had been left were gone. At first she was elated, but then got a sad little face. We asked her what was wrong. "I didn't get to see Santa come."

I told her it was okay, that he'd seen her and that was good enough. Then she smiled and grabbed up her first present.

Another Christmas at my parents home, I'd bought Dad's favorite cheese—Limburger. It has a pungent odor and taste, but oh did he ever love eating it. Mom, however, hated the smell as well as the taste. We had taken it down in the cooler and when we unpacked the food, someone saw that brightly colored package and stuck it under the tree.

Well, by the evening we started to smell something strange. The town they lived in had a refinery nearby and there was always a smell of it when the wind was just right. So we just passed *that* off as the culprit. We all went to bed and in the morning, as we came downstairs there was that strange smell again. Dad tracked it down to the tree. So after digging through the presents, we found this small package—sure enough, there was the cheese.

Mom said, "Get that out of here right now." So Dad took it to the kitchen and wrapped it in plastic wrap and threw it in the refrigerator. Mom wasn't happy about it, but what was really the end for her was when dad continue to eat some of it at the dinner table. We couldn't help but laugh and he put it away to eat it another day.

We also spent some special Christmases at Paul's parents. His mother alway had a good spread and she made the best fudge you ever wrapped your tongue around. Christmas was meager, there, and we met at his parent's small home, but there were a lot more kids like Donna and Mike to play with, and that was always fun for them.

As the years went by, things changed, again, and we found ourselves going to my cousin Rheta's home for Christmas. Our kids were the only ones there, but all the adult there were like a bunch of children as we got so engrossed with the food, especially my mom's Blueberry Rhubarb pie, Aunt Ruby's Southern Pecan Pie, and then the unwrapping of the gifts. We didn't unwrap them all at once. Oh, no. The tradition was to go around the room and each one of us would unwrap a present and then show it off to the sound of oh's and ah's.

We still do it today, but there are only a few of us left. We still love giving and receiving. As for me, I love watching the look on each face as they unwrap their gifts. We really enjoy it when it comes to our grandchildren, although we have only been with them a few times at Christmas. I still get quite a kick from it all. Christmas is for kids of all sizes and ages. It is a time of joy, celebrating, the new ones in the family, remembering those who have left us with wonderful stories that are carried down through the family. Yes, I wouldn't give Christmas up for anything in the world, especially for family ties that bind—and a piece of pie.

Left: Christmas at Grandpa and Grandma Huffman's.

Right: Christmas at cousin Rheta Cunningham-Dartts' home.

## Mildred Huffman's Never Fail Pie Crust

1 1/2 cups shortening
4 cups flour
1/2 cup cold water
1 tbsp. white vinegar
1 tbsp. sugar
1 tsp. salt
1 egg-beaten

Cut shorting in with flour and sugar. BEAT egg, water, vinegar and gradually ADD: to flour mixture and blend ingredients together, until a ball has been formed. Divide ball into four equal balls and roll out into crust from each ball. Fill with favorite filling and BAKE until golden brown. Makes 2 pies.

## Mildred Huffman's Blueberry Rhubarb Pie

2 cups blueberries-frozen

1 tsp. Cinnamon

1/2 cup water

1/3 cup water

3 tbsp. corn starch mixed with

2 cups fresh or frozen rhubarb-chopped

In a large pan COMBINE: rhubarb, sugar, 1/2 cup water and cinnamon. COOK over medium heat until this comes to a gentle boil, stirring so it won't stick. ADD: cornstarch, to 1/3 cup water and slowly stir this so it won't lump. When thickened, remove from heat and add blueberries. FOLD berries in gently and put filling into a prepared pie crust. Put top crust on, seal. Brush with a little cold water or beaten egg and sprinkle top with a pinch sugar. BAKE at 375° until pie is golden brown. To prevent edges of pie burning, cover with a little tin foil around the edges. Remove about ten minutes before pie is done.

*Note Recipe makes two pies. A pie for those who truly love blueberries. The extra addition of the rhubarb, which my mother put in makes this pie a wonderful dessert. A scoop of French vanilla ice cream really tops this off to please anyone's sweet tooth.

## Aunt Ruby's Southern Pecan Pie

1 cup white corn syrup
1 cup dark brown sugar
3 eggs
1/3 tsp. Salt
1/3 cup marg. or butter
1 tsp. Vanilla
1 cup pecans-chopped coarsely


MIX and POUR in unbaked pie shell. BAKE in 350° oven approximately 45-50 minutes. Every Christmas we all look forward to this sweet scrumptious pie. The special touch that Ruby puts into it makes it worth waiting for.


There are, of course, other holidays we've enjoyed and there is a special one that's become a joke around the dinner table. The kids must have been about seven and ten. We were at Mom and Dad's for Thanksgiving and the meal was going so well. Princess, was under the table, but no one thought about it until an awful odor came wafting up to out noses.

At first, Donna said Mike, "had let one," but then we heard a "pufftt" and realized it was the dog who'd gassed out.

"Oh, Princess you let a stinky," Mike scolded, at which Donna got the giggles and almost choked on her food.

Then Mom said, "Now kids, stop picking on poor Princess. She's old and can't help it.

That kind of quieted us all down and we finished our dinner with only an    iional smirk from the kids. There wasn't another incident. We still    'augh about it and I can't sit down for a meal at Mom's without checking under the table—even though Princess has long since passed away.

There have been a couple of outstanding winter holidays. One that comes to mind is the time we spent it at Donna and Owen's. We'd come back through from traveling to Arizona to see our grandchildren, son and daughter-in-law. It was Valentine's Day and neither Donna nor I had received anything from our respective spouses. Paul has always been good about getting me a flower or a nice card, but the guys were busy with a project Owen was working on. I don't remember if it was me giving Paul a card that morning or Donna mentioning that we would have lunch out, but soon after breakfast the guys said they had to go to the local home improvement store and also stop and get gas. So we cleaned up after breakfast and I went to make our bed. When the guys got back they had big smiles on their faces and we knew something was up. They told us to close our eyes and when we opened them, we saw two huge envelopes propped against the wall. I mean, they were huge.

Inside the big envelopes were beautiful cards. They also gave each of us a flower to plant. We were so surprised, we didn't know what to say, but we gave each of our hubby's a big hug and kiss. We did go out to lunch and had a great time. That was eight years ago, and I still have that card and every Valentine's Day I get it out and remember how special that day was for us. These sweet memories that last forever. We all need to have such things in our lives to keep us on the up side. It's times like these that give us the will to go on—knowing someone loves us.

The infamous Princess.

One year I decided to make my own card. I really love using those card applications on a computer, and I wrote this poem for my husband.

## My Sweetheart

Let me call you "My sweetheart"
On this Valentine's Day
To tell you that I cherish you
In every little way
To let you know I truly treasure,
All the little things you do
That makes it a sheer pleasure
Just sharing my life with you
And if I've forgotten to say "I love you" lately,
Then let me do so now
To tell you exactly why and how
It means so much to me
To let me call you, My sweetheart
What a special day this will be.

Now for the etc. Some occasions that fall under this category: weddings anniversaries, baptisms, births and deaths. In 2010, Paul and I celebrated our 50th wedding anniversary. We decided to have it at our home and though it's on the small side, we have a large dinning room and a lovely backyard. We worked hard on getting the backyard in top shape with beautiful plants and set up tables with umbrellas and spruced up our gazebo. When the day arrived, we had the food all set out on the dinning room table. It looked like it was going to be a wonderful experience, but shortly after some of the first guests had arrived I heard a familiar sound in the distance that sent my hair on end. It sounded like a rumble of thunder.

*Oh no*, I thought to myself. *The last thing we need is rain.* But we do live in Illinois, and you never know from morning to afternoon what our weather holds for us. All seemed to be going well, when a loud crack of thunder was heard much closer—then it all let loose at one time. It just poured down. People who where outside came running back into the dinning room through the sliding doors, and there were friends coming in the front door. All of a sudden my dinning room was packed with wall-to-wall people. Although the rain had ruined it outside, we all had a great time inside, and the whole evening turned out to be just wonderful. With good food, people talking and laughing, we had, again, formed sweet memories.

As I've already written about my wedding, and the births of my children have been told, but there was one birth that stands out in my mind that I shall not forget.

I had flown out to Arizona to watch our grandchildren while Kim and Mike had their last baby. The baby was expected the next week after I'd arrived. I'd come out a little early on purpose, so Kim's last week would be easier. The day after I got there we went to a children's function at church. When we got back Kim complained that her back was really bothering her. I had her lay down for a while and got the kids' lunch. I told Mike that she was going to have the baby that night.

He thought I was joking, but there are times when we women have a sixth sense, and you just know you're right. The evening came, and all the kids were in bed. I'd decided to sleep on the couch in the living room. I just had a feeling I needed to be there instead of the family room where I'd slept the night before. Around one or two in the morning, I was awakened with Mike saying, "Mom, we're going to the hospital. I think Kim is in labor."

"I knew it!" I said, "I was right."

"I guess so," Mike said. "Now we have got to get to that hospital. Will you make sure the kids get off to school and I'll call you when we know anything."

"Off you go now," I told him, and soon they were out the door and on their way to becoming parents for the fifth time.

I could barely get back to sleep, keeping one ear open and the phone near to me. I finally drifted off, and by early morning the phone rang. It was Mike announcing the birth of their new little boy—Adam Osborn. The kids were bouncing off the walls and none of them wanted to go to school, but I got them off. About that time Mike walked in with a big grin on his face. What a day that was! What joy there was! We talked for a few minutes and then he went to take a shower and catch a nap before he headed back to the hospital.

I'd never been able to be there for the other births. This was just the cherry on top of the big yummy ice-cream Sunday.

Adam has become the joyful one of the family with his infectious smile and laughter that just send thrills of happiness through you. It's such occasions that make a family.

We decided to have a special dinner the next day. We went to the store and bought some steaks and my granddaughter and I made a cake. After church, Mike took all the kids up to see their mommy and the new baby, When they got back Mike grilled the steaks and with a good salad and baked potato we all sat down to a wonderful meal. After the dishes were done, Mike took me up to meet our newest grandson, and oh how sweet he was. It was such a rush to hold Adam in my arms, and it made me so glad I was there. It's funny, but a new life just makes the world seem so much better. You might say that day, I had my cake and ate it too.

# The Horse Tank

Did you even wonder what became of good clean water? You know the kind you drink from a pure source? Now days it has to be cleaned, run through a process that takes all the minerals out, and then other stuff is put back in—just so we can drink it.

A few years ago we were driving down an old country road where I had lived as a child—a piece of land that had once belonged to my grandfather. As we got out of the car, I looked around and saw only weeds and ruins of what was once an old country home.

As I walked around, I saw the old tree that had grown at the side of the house and the old lilacs that still lined the rock driveway. Then I heard that familiar sound of running water and thought, *Could it be.* I walked over to the old horse tank and pulled away some of the weeds and yes—the water still ran cold and clear.

Dad and Mom had come with us, and I ask him if it was still safe to drink. "Are you kidding me?" Dad answered. "Of course it is. We still come here and get water from it and the donkeys that now live on this property drink from it."

I quickly went back to the car and found an empty water bottle. I turned the pipe around and out came clear, spring water—cold and fresh. I filled up the bottle, turned the pipe back around so it would flow into the old horse tank, and took a drink of what the best water I've ever tasted. "Oh, I wish I could take this home with me."

Dad said, "That can be arranged. We'll go back to our house and get some bottles." I sat down on an old step of the back porch and waited, reflecting on all the wonderful things that had happened on this property: the first time I saw Grandpa clean fish, how he killed chickens, gathering eggs.

I took another sip of my water. How great it tasted.

To think there was a time when that water was hauled by the bucket into the house, be it hot or freezing, Grandpa would do it. Then Grandma would heat the water and wash clothes or do dishes and cook with the water he hauled to the house in bucketsful. How spoiled we are today. Now that spring has been diverted from my grandparent's old place to another property across the road where a house has been built. We sometimes yearn for that same kind of fresh water to spring from a spiritual well to cleanse our souls and renew them. We have that, when we read good books, our scriptures, worship in our respective churches, say our prayers and take time to remember that someone greater than us loves us and is there to renew us with everlasting springs of spiritual waters.

The old horse tank on the Kirkpatrick farm
near where my friends, cousins and I made hollyhock dolls.

## Quilts and Stuff

There's nothing more comforting than a warm cup of cocoa and a comfortable quilt to wrap up in when the winter winds are knocking at your door. Quilts were such a part of our lives when I was a girl. Mom, her sisters and Grandma would get together and make a quilt for someone who'd had a baby, or a someone who was getting married. Each quilt was different, depending on the person who was to receive it. Before I was born, my grandmother made a quilt called the wedding-ring quilt. What a beautiful quilt is was and still is today. Every detail was perfection. She didn't have a fancy electric sewing machine that can make all kinds of stitches and patterns like folks do today. She did have an old foot peddle Singer that you pumped by your foot to keep it going, but the quilts were usually made by hand.

I know the quilt she made for me was a labor of love as she handstitched the pieces together. Then she sat a quilt frame that the quilt was stretched across and rolled from side to side as those who sat around it quilted with small stitches making patterns that turned each quilt into a piece of art.

When I got married, Mother made me a beautiful Dutch Girl quilt. We had it for many years and unfortunately until it was damaged in a fire and was unsalvageable. Later on, she made me another beautiful quilt that I treasure.

My mother-in-law Betty made us a couple of quilts—one of which hangs over our bed on a wall rack. Quilts were also made for our daughter and son when they got married. Mother's love of sewing made them especially wonderful. I think the one thing Mom would say she'd liked to do, now that she's in her 90s and almost blind—is if she could have one wish, it would be to see again so she could quilt and knit.

Among those things taught by my grandmother to her daughters was the art of knitting. Mom took right to it and knitted the most beautiful afghans. Unfortunately knitting and sewing aren't things I enjoy—although I learned to quilt and have done a few, including one for our bed that my friend Mary helped me put together. I do love to crochet. A few years ago Mother made her last quilt for her last great grandson—at that time her eye sight would not allow her to sew any more. Some might say, such a shame that she can no longer make the quilts, but I say all those quilts, afghans, knitted vests, and shawls are her legacy to her children, grandchildren and great grand children. They are treasures of skill, love and diligence—and must be measured by the heart. As the following poem states:

## The Quilter

In the light of the lantern near
She stitches the material for someone dear,
As the patterns skillfully appear, colors rich and bright
The Quilter work into the night
And as the lantern dies down,
She lays aside her piece of work
Only to pick it up at the next day's light
Each stitch is a labor of love
Given by the hand of God above
Until at last the quilt is done
And the words "Victory has been won."
Have been carefully stitched
Around the ends of the a beautiful piece
She names: The Victory Quilt

# Garden, Birds and Bees

One of the things I've enjoyed over the years is my garden. Both my husband and I have worked in it, and have made so many changes from a Strawberry trailing garden in the back corner, to a water pond feature, to where now a lovely statue, with flowers around it, standing in the middle of the little garden hill. That part of the garden always seemed to be a problem until my husband worked his handy, magic fingers on the garden. Over the years we've had a peach tree, which we enjoyed, but had to share with the local squirrels—even though we didn't want to. We had an ash tree that grew and shaded our house. In it lived various birds and my favorite little wrens would be there every spring to occupy the little birdhouse Dad build for us.

One day, when I went out to my garden to work, I saw something crawling through the grass—a snake! Our little dog Mindi barked and barked until the snake finally turned the other way and crawled back into another yard.

Another day I looked out my back window and sitting on the fence was the biggest bird I'd ever seen. As I opened the sliding glass doors to get a better look, it lifted in flight and settled in the neighbor's tree. I got out my binoculars and identified it as a white heron. I called the local forest preserve and they sent out the naturalist from the University of Illinois. They came out and found a pair of them at the local creek.

One morning I found a deer in the backyard drinking from the pond. It was there until something spooked it and it ran off. It seemed so strange as we live in a subdivision, however that area still has corn and wheat fields near by. I love sitting watching my birds: cardinals, purple and yellow finches, nuthatches, wrens, and hummingbirds. I get a wonderful show all summer.

We have changed the garden again. Not to long ago, we had to cut down our wonderful ash tree, because of the ash-tree disease working it's way into our area. It was already showing signs of stress, so we cut it down. It was a sorry time for us. We didn't want to lose that tree. Without it, our birds would have to find another place to roust. As the limbs were being cut off, we heard a cracking sound—then a loud boom! Before I knew it, a tree limb was sticking down through our roof.

"What in the world happened." I asked Paul.

"It seems they misjudged the limb and it turned on them and broke too soon. Now we have a hole in the roof and in our dining-room ceiling."

On top of everything else, it was beginning to rain. I envisioned our dinning room in a pool of deep water.

I have to hand the applause to the man who cut the tree down, though. Not only did he cover the roof on a temporary basis, but that night he came back over and patched the roof in the attic, fixed and patched the ceiling in the dining room, and spackled and painted the ceiling for us. Last year we had to have the a new roof put on and there was that patch. It had held well and prevented us from having a leak or two.

Although the tree's gone, and will be missed, my house is safe from falling limbs. Now we have a lovely raised garden in place of the tree, and a water feature that sounds so lovely. It invites the birds to come drink and I can still sit out on the patio and watch them. As for my wrens, we bought a very tall shepherds-crook hanger and we hung up the wren house—hoping they would find it. Winter came, then spring and every day I watched to see if the birdhouse was occupied. Then one day, I heard a familiar sound. Could it be? I carefully looked out the window of my kitchen and there—sitting at the top of my water feature—was a tiny wren. His song vibrated tough the morning air. I was elated to hear that little bird singing. Now, two years later, they're still coming back to the house and I look forward to seeing those little heads popping in and out as they lay their eggs and when the new little wrens start squawking for mommy and daddy to feed them. In this poem below I reflect my love for my garden.

## In My Garden

In my garden where flowers bloom
There's never a dull moment
Nor is there any gloom
There are butterflies and hummingbirds
and only the softest sounds are heard
It's lovely and peaceful and oh so tranquil
Why, there's a mother Robin with a worm in her bill
I love to sit and read amongst my flowers,
and before I know it, the minutes have turned into hours
The colors are so lovely and so bright
As dew sparkles in the morning light
I come to my garden when I am sad,
and natures own beauty makes me glad
It's nature at it's very best
Won't you come in and be my guest?

# Dogs, Cats and Other Creatures

When I was a little girl we had a dog. She was a Border-Collie mix. She was by my side a lot when we went out to the barn, garden or pasture.

I vaguely remember little things about this dog, but mainly that it was there for me, though we didn't keep her too long because she ate too much.

We didn't have any other dogs, but Grandpa had a German Shepard mix that was extraordinary. He trained it to fetch cows from the pasture. I think he called it Shep. All he had to do was give a whistle and the dog would do his bidding.

He also had cows, cats and mice. Of course the cats were there to catch the mice and for their job well done my grandfather would give them milk. Now he didn't just give it in a bowl, oh, no. They would wait for him to come milk and when he sat down, they would line up and as he milked he would squirt milk from the cows udder and into each cats mouth. I do wish I had a picture of that. What a sight it was!

One of my most treasured animal was a cat named Suzybelle. She was a gray/brown and black-striped cat—most likely an American tabby. I loved that cat so much. When we moved from the farm, she had to go with us. As an only child, the aspect of moving from my secure surroundings of the farm to an unfamiliar place—with no knowledge of what to expect—really shook me up. That cat got me through the move. You might say she was my security blanket. I'd sleep with her and take her outside with me to sit and read. One day, after I got home from school, I looked for her. She wasn't in her usual place in the sun, napping. I called for her. Mom said she'd seen her walking beyond the garden. I went out there and looked but couldn't find her. Later that day Dad found her laying in the weeds. She has passed away. Cats will go off like that when they know their time has come—as do some dogs. They take their last walk, so to speak, which leads them to cat or dog heaven. I cannot begin to tell you what a loss that was for me. I mourned for her just as I would any dear friend that passes on. In time we had other animals and they were fun, but there would never be another Suzybelle.

Years later, just before I was to get married, Mom and Dad got a little Boston terrier. She was cute as a button and was a great companion for them. I grew to love her, too, for the short time I was home. She proved to be a devoted pet.

When our son was younger, we had many little creatures around the house, a fish in a bowl, a turtle, Gerbils and Charlie. Charlie was a guinea pig and whatever inspired me to let our son have one eludes me now. However, he begged for one and we gave in. At first he was fun. Mike would put him in a clear plastic "running" ball and that little creature would run around the house. We told our son that he was responsible for the feeding and cleaning of the cage Charlie stayed in.

One day when I was in the kitchen and had opened the refrigerator door, I heard this loud squeaking noise. As I got out the carrots, celery, lettuce to make a salad the noise got louder. I soon learned that every time you opened the refrigerator door, Charlie would squeak and run crazily around his cage. It was a bit unnerving, and when we had to go on a two-week vacation we told Mike to find another home for Charlie on a temporary basis. He did. But when we got back, Mike decided he didn't need Charlie and shortly after, we got a dog.

After Charlie, we did decided the kids were old enough to be responsible for a dog and so when the dog across the street had babies we got one. She was a crazy-looking dog. And as she grew up, she wasn't the prettiest dog around. She was, well, ugly and yet she was a cute little dog in an odd way.

She was the whelp of a mix between a pure-bred Miniature Poodle and a Dachshund. We named her Cinderella, but called her "Cindy" for short. She was a long-haired dog, and we did out best to train her. She did fairly well, but she had a temper, and you couldn't touch her precious bone she chewed on without her growling at you. As she got older, she became feeble and died. We buried her in our backyard. Shortly after we had buried her, our son was walking past the backdoor and said he could have sworn he heard her whining and scratching at the door, just as she had done may a time, but when he opened the door there was nothing there.

A little while later, we saw an ad in the paper for dogs being given away. My daughter and I drove down to the place and we came back with the most adorable little black dog with a small, white blaze on her chest. We named her Mindi-dog, but mostly she was called Mindi. Right off the bat we knew there was something special about this dog. We were right. As we were taking her home, Donna had put her on a pillow on her lap. There was a storm brewing and as the lightning flashed and thunder rolled around us, we thought this little puppy would be afraid, but she slept right through it. I think it was Donna's voice talking that started her off right. As she grew up Donna had a way of training her that stuck. She became a companion to all of us. She loved Mike to pieces, would sit by Paul in his big lounge chair and lay by my side when I was sick.

She was so smart. One day we had company, and we hadn't been paying much attention to her, She trotted in with her water bowl and dropped it at my feet. Well, was I surprised as were our guests. After that incident, whenever her bowl was dry she'd pick it up, and trot around in the house until she found us and drop it at our feet. She was a fierce squirrel hunter in the backyard. All you had to say was, "Mindi, Squirrel," and let her out the door. She would go tearing out into the yard. Then when she saw them, she'd go crazy barking and trying to jump up the trees to get them. She even tried to cling to a tree one time. One winter she saw a squirrel and when we let her out, she took off only to find the snow was too slick and she and the squirrel went sliding clear to the back fence where she hit it just as the wiley creature she was chasing scooted up the fence, taking time to sit up there and give her, what I would call, a squirrel snicker.

That didn't stop her from chasing them and even as she got old she still found enough steam to chase them once in a while. As the kids left home, we became Mindi's sole companions and when we went out for the first time to visit our son in Arizona, she went right along with us.

As she grew older she, too, became burdened with pain and problems. She got hit by car, and fell and hurt her back in two separate occasions. Eventually we had to make the hard decision to put her down. We put her in a special casket my husband built and when we buried her. The other dogs that knew her howled and cried, as if they knew what had happened. After that we never got another dog or cat—although I still love animals very much.

I do think that having an animal in your home is a good thing, if you can. It adds a sense of security. Even a cat can sense danger and warn you. I'm not saying everyone should have a dog or cat, but there's a great need for homes for them and someday we'll have another one in our home. There have been studies proving that having an animal in your home, helps you be healthier, happier and even safer in some cases.

There are service dogs for the blind and handicapped that become invaluable to those who need them. I have to say, I "Man's best friend is his dog," may be true. As for me, I'll never forget the joy, and happiness they've given me.

Shortly after Mindi's passing I wrote a little poem dedicated to all dogs. I dedicate it to Princess, Suzybelle, Cindy, Mindi-dog, Ruby and all those dogs and cats that need homes. Here is a portion of that poem:

They say that all dogs go to heaven.
And this I do believe
For I saw it in a dream one night
As real as real could be
I walked through a field of gold & greens
Where puppies and dogs did run and play
And all of it seemed so right
As I saw you running up to me
With your ears flapping in the wind
You lick my hand in a gentle way
Then before I knew it the night turned to day.

On occasion now and then we doggie-sit Ruby, a spunky little Dachshund. She's just crazy about chasing birds, squirrel and anything else. She's also so bold she will challenge a dog three times her size and her owners told us she killed a snake once. My hats off to you, brave little dog. I can't help but sing the song. "Oh Ruby, Don't Take Your Love From Me" for she does tug at my heart strings.

Above is Mindi-Dog.

At left: Suzybelle cat.

# Cops and Robbers

In the 1930s there was a very bad man in Chicago, Illinois, by the name of Al Capone. He lived in Maywood, near Chief of Police H.R. Bailey's Cicero precinct, and H.R. Bailey was my husband Paul's grandfather.

There were many time when Al Capone's gang would fight with other gangs. It was on such an occasion that Paul's Grandfather Harold R. Bailey had a run-in with one of Capone's gang.

We don't know the exact details, but we do know there was a shootout and Chief Bailey was shot in the line of duty. The bullet passed through his body—just missing his heart. Though it was a near-death experience, he was taken to a near-by hospital where he was treated and a short time later, was sent home. It was a dreadful time, though, for his children and wife Anna. He received several Stars for his service and heroism in the line of duty to his community. He later retired with honors and moved to California.

H.R. Bailey
Chicago, Illinois,
1930s.

# From Pastor to Pasture

Recently, my father, at the age of ninety-two, decided to retire from the little church where he'd first preached and was returned to 50 years later. He served at the Farmers Chapel Methodist Church for six years—until Sunday, June 26, 2011—when he preached his last sermon. As we all sat there and listened to him I realized there was "snow on the mountain" but there was still fire in his soul. It was a beautiful sermon and as he finished, the thought came to me that someone like my dad, "Rev. Glenn" as most folk call him, has been a devoted messenger of God's word and would never really retire as he will go on being the shining example of a devoted servant of the Lord. It was he and Mother that made the difference. She was faithfully by his side all the way, and though she suffered much illness, she still supported him in his calling as a minister for all those years.

How can we be that same way? No matter what or who, no matter which faith we are, we can be a shinning example. In some ways it was an era ending for Dad, but it was a beginning for him and Mom. Now they could devote time to each other. I doubt Dad will ever stop being a minister for he will always be "Rev. Glenn" to all those who know him. Mom will always be "Mrs.Huffman" the woman at his side.

Do pastors ever go to pasture? The answer is a resounding "No." For all who are Pastors, Minsters, Bishops, Missionaries or Prophets, whoever they may be, will always be in the service of their God.

# Black Smoke and Peanut Butter Sandwiches

Now I close this book with this one last story—a story I wrote for a project in my college class. Although it was written as a fiction—most of is based on facts. It may seem as if I repeat myself in a few areas, but it's the inspiration for my book and you'll see why I left this one for my last story.

One day I was visiting Mom and Dad. My husband had gone out to help Dad in the garden, so I decided this would be a great time to ask Mom about my early years. "Mom, what was it like when I was a little girl?" I asked, sitting in her comfortable living room, with a small tape recorder in her hand. "I've been reminiscing about my childhood but there are some things I just don't remember. Can you help me out?"

"Oh my," Mother replied, rolling her eyes. "you were a bit of a handful when you young."

"Okay," I said with a sigh. "Let's have it.

As we talked I realized there was very little remembered about my early childhood and most of it was bits and pieces.

Mom began, "Well, first off when I met your father he worked at shoe factory for $16.00 a week and I worked at The Box in Danville, Illinois, and made $8.00 a week. We were married in 1939. In 1941 you were born and the same year the Japanese bombed Pearl Harbor. It became part of our history as well as being written in the history books.

"It was late in the summer of 1944 and war time. Looking back it seems impossible that a small country girl like you from Illinois would be even remotely affected by all of it. Like many men in our nation, your father was called to serve his country. He went into the Air Force and was shipped from air base to air base, and we would follow him. We would barely get settled into one place and then have to move. It was during this time that we had some unusual experiences. One of those was during that summer when your father was shipped to the Air Force base in Galveston, Texas. We were to follow after him when he found a place for us to live.

"We were lucky to have been escorted by your uncle, who had to ride a train to another destination. He saw to it that we were on the right train. If it hadn't been for him we would have never made it on the train going to Houston, Texas. The St. Louis station was packed so full of people mingling ever which way that one could have easily gotten lost. When the conductor called, 'All aboard,' your uncle grabbed you up under his arm like a sack of potatoes, picked up the largest of the three suitcases we had and made a beeline for the train. He was a tall man and as he hurried I could see his head bobbing amongst the crowd."

Mom stopped for minute, poured two glasses of lemonade, then went on to tell her story as I listened with great interest.

"Hurry, Mildred, or we won't make it," your Uncle Ray called to me.

"I'm coming!" I hollered over the din of other passenger as they clambered to get to the train also."

Mother, who barely weighed 100 pounds, followed him as closely as she could hanging on to the last two suitcases.

Mother continued, "People piled on as fast as they could and I was almost crushed in the rush. Once on the train, your uncle grabbed a seat for us and we both plopped down in it. He put two of the bags in the overhead and stuffed the smaller one under the seat. If we had not gotten a seat we would have had to sit on our suitcases in the isles until a seat came available at the next stop. Even at that, it would have been like playing musical chairs to be the first to grab a seat.

"Uncle Ray gave us both a quick hug and some instructions of safety, then quickly left us to catch his train going a different direction. We watched him wave goodbye from the platform. It seemed like such a final wave."

As I looked back on this time, I began to remember the feeling of excitement of being on a train.

"Go on."

"I hadn't wanted to leave Grandma and Grandpa and the little home we lived in near them.

"Not long after we had settled into our one seat, the woman across from us introduced herself. She was a very nice lady whose husband was also stationed in Texas. The train picked up speed and it clipped along passing farms, little towns and cities. Sometimes it would stop to let people on and off. The train became very hot, muggy and crowded. It was lucky for us that the lady across the seat from us was willing to hold our seat while we went for potty breaks and we did the same for her. Later in the trip, when I realized that there was no way we could get any food, the lady shared some food with us. With your tummy full, you curled up on my lap and fell asleep, leaving me to look out the window at the passing scenery. That didn't last long. It was so hot, humid and sticky in the section we were in that many of the windows had to be opened to get some air in. Much to my dismay it also let in the smoke pouring from the engine as it billowed backwards.

"It covered us all with a thin film of smoke dust making everyone look like a bad imitation of *Uncle Tom's Cabin*. I tried to clean us both up, but it only made it worse and finally settled for just trying to keep your face fairly clean. It didn't help any that you had to sit on my lap most of the time. I attempted to get some sleep, but with a restless three-year-old, that was near to impossible."

"Oh Mom, how awful that must have been." I sat down my glass of lemonade on a nearby table and went over and gave her a hug.

"Well, that was just a drop in the bucket." Mom replied. "A day later, after a bad incident, we reached Houston, Texas, then made our way to a bus station. It was there that I was able to get us cleaned up enough to continue our trip. As we arrived in Galveston it was almost midnight and there wasn't a soul waiting for us. By this time I was at my wits end. With no husband in sight, and no one there I knew, it made me even more anxious. We stood on the platform for the longest time, hoping to see your father.

"Finally the bus driver, who was just getting off from his shift, took pity on us. After a bit of a search he finally found the only taxi that was available, and it had to be shared with three other women—plus all the baggage. Our suitcases, were thrown into the trunk and on top of the carrier.

"The driver climbed into his seat and said, "Everyone ready?" And off we all went. After a crowded ride around town, while others were dropped off, the taxi was left to us. We finally stopped outside a small, dark apartment building. At the curb shone a dim street light.

"We had reached our destination. The driver stopped the car, got out, dumped our suitcases on the sidewalk and said, That'll be five bucks lady. I paid him and we and our baggage were left at the curb to fend for ourselves. I hauled the bags to the stairs inside and saw by the mailbox label that showed our apartment was on the third floor."

Mom stopped for a moment, took a sip of lemonade and continued, "I looked up those stairs with a very heavy sigh, and began to trudge up the dimly lit stairs to the third floor with the first two bags, leaving you on the first step with the last bag. Once the bags were dumped at the door, I came back to get you and the other suitcase. You were half asleep, hanging on to the last suitcase for a pillow. As we climbed those three flights of stairs I wondered outloud, 'Why did I agree to come here? I must have been out of my mind.' After getting the door unlocked, I half-kicked, half-pushed the suitcases into the apartment. Slamming the door shut, I said, 'I hope I didn't wake anyone up.'

"You looked up at me from where I had set you down and said, 'I'm hungry Mommy.'

"I answered wearily, 'So am I. It's been a long time since we ate yesterday. I wish your father was here to help.' I gave you a weak smile."

"I walked slowly into the tiny, cramped kitchen to check for food and saw a note from your father: 'Sorry dear, but had to get back to the base before curfew time. Hope you made it safely here. Love you both, Glenn.' "

Mom paused again, shifted her tiny body in the rocking chair and continued, "There was only a quart of milk and some juice in the fridge. He'd just enough time to quickly go to a small grocery, nearby. He wouldn't be allow off base until morning; when he could then move in with us.

"So there I sat in an unfamiliar place in a strange city with a tired, hungry little child pulling at my skirt. It was enough to make anyone cry and that's exactly what I did." Mom said, pausing for a moment.

"Wow! That had to be the pits." I said.

"After I stopped crying and got our faces washed, we unpacked the first of the suitcases and there inside it was a small box tucked carefully amongst the clothing, with a note on top that read: 'You'll need this sometime on your trip. Love Mom & Dad Kirkpatrick.' Inside the box were two peanut butter and jelly sandwiches wrapped in double waxed paper. It was like getting a Christmas present in the summer. Even though they were a couple of days old they washed down with a glass of milk just fine.

"We ate them with great relish. As if they were a true gourmet meal," Mother exclaimed, chuckling.

"After we were full, on went on your 'jammies,'and I put you into a large baby bed that had mistakenly been provided for you. I made the big bed up and climbed into it—sinking down into the clean sheets I'd brought. With good nights said, we both fell asleep from sheer exhaustion."

"Yes, I remember that," I replied. "The only thing I could think of was seeing my daddy the next day. Thanks so much, Mom, for this step back in time. It's meant a lot to me and getting it on tape is even better!"

I checked the tape recorder and when I looked up, Mother had fallen asleep. I continue to reflect I continue to reflect and on the tape recording I made, and I finished with this last statement of the afternoon: "Certain sounds and fragrances bring back floods of memories, but none so poignant and as simple as the smell of black smoke and peanut butter sandwiches."

—Photo courtesy of Mark Rosebrough

A Family Portrait at Great-Grandparents, Glenn and Mildred Huffman's 70th Wedding Anniversary—2009.
From left—Adults: Kimberly and Michael Osborn, Glenn Huffman, Mildred Huffman, Paul and Valerie Osborn, Donna and Owen Hemmert
Children, left center: Austin, Glenn, and Shayla Osborn
Front Row: Adam and Jeffrey Osborn.

—Donna Hemmert, photographer

Valerie and Paul Osborn—sweethearts since 1960,
with Donna and Owen's Bobbi-cat.
Donna and Owen Hemmert's home in Texas.

Other biographies, family histories and memoirs published
by Mayhaven Publishing, Inc.


*95 Years With John "Jack" Day* by John "Jack" Day
*Abraham Lincoln: From Skeptic to Prophet* by Wayne C. Temple
*Bailey Island: Memories Pictures and Lore* by Nancy Orr Johnson Jensen
*Bittersweet: A Daughter's Memoir* by Marilyn Arnold
*Black Smoke & Peanut Butter Sandwiches* by Valerie Huffman Osborn
*Blaw Hunter, Blaw Thy Horn* by Gary Forrester
*Brother Mine Lessons Learned* by Mike Odell
*Chicken Tommy & Other Stories* by Richard Thomas
*Dear Family* by Marjorie Heaton Lynn
*General James W. Singleton: Lincoln's Mysterious Copperhead Ally* by Peter J. Barry
*Long Story Short* by Nancy Easter Schick
*Rose Haven Farm* by Katherine "Kit" Inman
*Sister & Me* by Gertrude Stonesifer
*Still a Country Boy After Embracing the World* by Loren Finnell
*Sugar From Lettuce* by Marjorie Heaton Lynn
*Ten Sisters: A True Story* by the Ten Sisters
*To Send A Dove: One Woman's Triumph over Breast Cancer* by Delorse H. Rutherford
*Two Walk the Golden Road* by Wilson Powell & Zhou Ming